BASIC UNDERSTANDING OF THE TOEIC® L&R TEST

Masaaki Ogura

JN126085

KINSEIDO

Kinseido Publishing Co., Ltd.

3-21 Kanda Jimbo-cho, Chiyoda-ku,
Tokyo 101-0051, Japan

First published 2022 by Kinseido Publishing Co., Ltd.

Cover design: Takayuki Minegishi
Text design & Editorial support: C-leps Co., Ltd.
Writing support: George Whalley
                 Johnny Driggs
                 Shari J. Berman

音声ファイル無料ダウンロード

http://www.kinsei-do.co.jp/download/4155

この教科書で 🎧 DL 00 の表示がある箇所の音声は、上記 URL または QR コードにて
無料でダウンロードできます。自習用音声としてご活用ください。

▶ PC からのダウンロードをお勧めします。スマートフォンなどでダウンロードされる場合は、
　ダウンロード前に「解凍アプリ」をインストールしてください。
▶ URL は、検索ボックスではなくアドレスバー (URL 表示覧) に入力してください。
▶ お使いのネットワーク環境によっては、ダウンロードできない場合があります。

🔘 **CD 00**　左記の表示がある箇所の音声は、教室用 CD（Class Audio CD）に収録されています。

はじめに

　本書は *TOEIC*® Listening & Reading Test（以下 TOEIC L&R）の入門書として作成されました。TOEIC L&R は受けたことがない、受けたことがあるけれどあまり点数が良くなかった——そういった学習者が効率よく TOEIC L&R を攻略できるように工夫されています。本書では中学校・高校で学んできた英語の基礎を、TOEIC L&R に出題されやすいポイントに絞っておさらいし、スコアアップを狙うアプローチをとります。これまでに皆さんが学習してきたことがそのまま TOEIC L&R 攻略に直結します。その上で、試験に必要な知識を習得し、習得した知識を実践演習で得点に変えることができるように構成しました。

◎試験に必要な知識を習得する

　試験に必要な知識は、二つあります。一つが試験の全体像（形式や雰囲気）に関する知識。もう一つがよく出題される項目に関する知識です。前者については、十分に慣れることが必要です。TOEIC L&R 対策をする際に、問題形式だけが TOEIC L&R に類似しているというのでは意味はありません。よく出題されるトピック・ストーリーを厳選し、効率よく慣れることができるようにしました。後者については、きっと知らないものがたくさん掲載されているでしょう。しかし、心配ありません。よくある場面の中で頻出文法、語句・表現を学び、自然と身に付けられるように配置を工夫しています。それぞれのユニットを繰り返しよく学習すれば自然と、「この単語、見たことある！」と感じることが増えてくるでしょう。

◎習得した知識を実践演習で得点に変える

　単元ごとに学習しているときはできるけれど、試験本番ではうまくいかない——そういった経験はよくあることでしょう。単元ごとに学習した知識が身に付いているか確認し、本番での得点につなげるためには、ランダムな演習が重要です。本書では、Review Test を 2 回分用意しました。本番さながらの問題に取り組んで、弱点を洗い出し、復習することで、無駄なくスコアアップを狙います。

　本書が皆さんの TOEIC L&R のスコアアップと、実践的英語力の養成につながれば、これに勝る喜びはありません。

小倉雅明

本書は CheckLink（チェックリンク）対応テキストです。

CheckLink のアイコンが表示されている設問は、CheckLink に対応しています。

CheckLink を使用しなくても従来通りの授業ができますが、特色をご理解いただき、授業活性化のためにぜひご活用ください。

CheckLink の特色について

大掛かりで複雑な従来の e-learning システムとは異なり、CheckLink のシステムは大きな特色として次の 3 点が挙げられます。

1. これまで行われてきた教科書を使った授業展開に大幅な変化を加えることなく、専門的な知識なしにデジタル学習環境を導入することができる。
2. PC 教室や CALL 教室といった最新の機器が導入された教室に限定されることなく、普通教室を使用した授業でもデジタル学習環境を導入することができる。
3. 授業中での使用に特化し、教師・学習者双方のモチベーション・集中力をアップさせ、授業自体を活性化することができる。

▶教科書を使用した授業に「デジタル学習環境」を導入できる

本システムでは、学習者は教科書の CheckLink のアイコンが表示されている設問に PC やスマートフォン、アプリからインターネットを通して解答します。そして教師は、授業中にリアルタイムで解答結果を把握し、正解率などに応じて有効な解説を行うことができるようになっています。教科書自体は従来と何ら変わりはありません。解答の手段として CheckLink を使用しない場合でも、従来通りの教科書として使用して授業を行うことも、もちろん可能です。

▶教室環境を選ばない

従来の多機能な e-learning 教材のように学習者側の画面に多くの機能を持たせることはせず、「解答する」ことに機能を特化しました。PC だけでなく、一部タブレット端末やスマートフォン、アプリからの解答も可能です。したがって、PC 教室や CALL 教室といった大掛かりな教室は必要としません。普通教室でも CheckLink を用いた授業が可能です。教師は PC だけでなく、一部タブレット端末やスマートフォンからも解答結果の確認をすることができます。

▶授業を活性化するための支援システム

本システムは予習や復習のツールとしてではなく、授業中に活用されることで真価を発揮する仕組みになっています。CheckLink というデジタル学習環境を通じ、教師と学習者双方が授業中に解答状況などの様々な情報を共有することで、学習者はやる気を持って解答し、教師は解答状況に応じて効果的な解説を行う、という好循環を生み出します。CheckLink は、普段の授業をより活力のあるものへと変えていきます。

上記 3 つの大きな特色以外にも、掲示板などの授業中に活用できる機能を用意しています。従来通りの教科書としても使用はできますが、ぜひ CheckLink の機能をご理解いただき、普段の授業をより活性化されたものにしていくためにご活用ください。

CheckLink の使い方

CheckLink は、PC や一部のタブレット端末、スマートフォン、アプリを用いて、この教科書にある
ᑕ CheckLink のアイコン表示のある設問に解答するシステムです。
・初めて CheckLink を使う場合、以下の要領で**「学習者登録」**と**「教科書登録」**を行います。
・一度登録を済ませれば、あとは毎回**「ログイン画面」**から入るだけです。CheckLink を使う
　教科書が増えたときだけ、改めて**「教科書登録」**を行ってください。

CheckLink URL

https://checklink.kinsei-do.co.jp/student/

登録は **CheckLink 学習者用
アプリ**が便利です。ダウン
ロードはこちらから ▶ ▶ ▶

▶学習者登録 （PC ／タブレット／スマートフォンの場合）

①上記 URL にアクセスすると、右のページが表示されます。学校名を入力し
　「ログイン画面へ」を選択してください。
　PC の場合は「PC 用はこちら」**を選択して** PC 用ページを表示します。同
　様に学校名を入力し「ログイン画面へ」を選択してください。
②ログイン画面が表示されたら「初めての方はこちら」を選択し
　「学習者登録画面」に入ります。

③自分の学籍番号、氏名、メールアドレス（学校
　のメールなど**PC メールを推奨**）を入力し、次
　に**任意のパスワード**を 8 桁以上 20 桁未満（半
　角英数字）で入力します。なお、学籍番号は
　パスワードとして使用することはできません。
④「パスワード確認」は、❸で入力したパスワー
　ドと同じものを入力します。
⑤最後に「登録」ボタンを選択して登録は完了
　です。次回からは、「ログイン画面」から学籍
　番号とパスワードを入力してログインしてく
　ださい。

▶教科書登録

① ログイン後、メニュー画面から「教科書登録」を選び（PCの場合はその後「新規登録」ボタンを選択）、「教科書登録」画面を開きます。

② 教科書と受講する授業を登録します。
教科書の最終ページにある、**教科書固有番号**のシールをはがし、印字された**16桁の数字とアルファベット**を入力します。

③ 授業を担当される先生から連絡された**11桁の授業ID**を入力します。

④ 最後に「登録」ボタンを選択して登録は完了です。

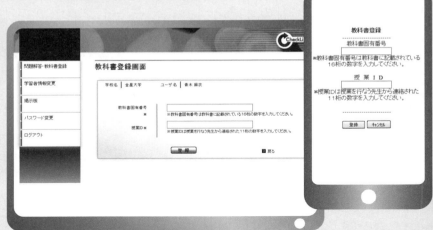

⑤ 実際に使用する際は「教科書一覧」（PCの場合は「教科書選択画面」）の該当する教科書名を選択すると、「問題解答」の画面が表示されます。

▶問題解答

① 問題は教科書を見ながら解答します。この教科書の ⟳CheckLink の アイコン表示のある設問に解答できます。

② 問題が表示されたら選択肢を選びます。

③ 表示されている問題に解答した後、「解答」ボタンを選択すると解答が登録されます。

▶CheckLink 推奨環境

PC

推奨 OS
　　Windows 7, 10 以降
　　MacOS X 以降

推奨ブラウザ
　　Internet Explorer 8.0 以上
　　Firefox 40.0 以上
　　Google Chrome 50 以上
　　Safari

携帯電話・スマートフォン
　　3G 以降の携帯電話（docomo, au, softbank）
　　iPhone, iPad（iOS9 ～）
　　Android OS スマートフォン、タブレット

・最新の推奨環境についてはウェブサイトをご確認ください。
・上記の推奨環境を満たしている場合でも、機種によってはご利用いただけない場合もあります。また、
　推奨環境は技術動向等により変更される場合があります。

▶CheckLink 開発

CheckLink は奥田裕司 福岡大学教授、正興 IT ソリューション株式会社、株式会社金星堂に
よって共同開発されました。

CheckLink は株式会社金星堂の登録商標です。

CheckLink の使い方に関するお問い合わせは…

正興ITソリューション株式会社　CheckLink 係

e-mail checklink@seiko-denki.co.jp

CONTENTS

Review Test マークシート

TOEIC® Listening & Reading Testについて

TOEIC は Test of English for International Communication の略で、英語コミュニケーション能力を測定する試験です。試験には複数の種類があり、全体としては*TOEIC*® Program と呼ばれます。

TOEIC® Program	
TOEIC® Tests	*TOEIC Bridge*® Tests
・**Listening & Reading Test** ・Speaking & Writing Test ・Speaking Test	・Listening & Reading Test ・Speaking & Writing Test

本書はこのうち、太字で表された Listening & Reading Test の学習を目的とします。
リスニング約45分間（100問）とリーディング75分間（100問）のテストで、マークシート方式です。問題は全て英語で構成されています。5点刻みのスコアで評価され、10 ～ 990 点のスコアが与えられます。

リスニングセクション：約45分間（100問） *音声は全て1度しか放送されません。音声は、アメリカ、イギリス、カナダ、オーストラリアの発音です。	
Part 1	**写真描写問題：6問** ・1枚の写真について4つの短い説明文を聞き、写真を最も的確に描写しているものを選ぶ。 ・説明文は印刷されていない。
Part 2	**応答問題：25問** ・1つの発言に対する3つの応答を聞き、最もふさわしいものを選ぶ。 ・発言と応答は印刷されていない。
Part 3	**会話問題：39問** ［1つの会話に3設問×13セット］ ・2人または3人による会話を聞き、設問に対する4つの選択肢から最も適切なものを選ぶ。 ・図表問題（会話中の情報と、印刷された図表などの情報を関連づけて解答）もある。 ・会話は印刷されていない。
Part 4	**説明文問題：30問** ［1つの説明文に3設問×10セット］ ・アナウンスなど、単一の発話者による説明文を聞き、設問に対する4つの選択肢から最も適切なものを選ぶ。 ・図表問題（説明文の情報と、印刷された図表などの情報を関連づけて解答）もある。 ・説明文は印刷されていない。

リーディングセクション：75分間（100問）		
Part 5	**短文穴埋め問題：30問** ・文の一部が空所になっており、そこに入る語（句）として最も適切なものを、4つの選択肢から選ぶ。	
Part 6	**長文穴埋め問題：16問**［1つの文書に4設問×4セット］ ・1つの文書の中に4つの空所があり、それぞれに入る語（句）や文として最も適切なものを4つの選択肢から選ぶ。	
Part 7	**文章理解問題：54問** 1つの文書：29問［1つの文書に2〜4設問×10セット］ 複数の文書：25問［2〜3つの文書に5設問×5セット］ ・Eメールや求人情報、記事、広告、チャットでのやりとりなど、多岐にわたる内容の文書を読み、それに関する設問に答える。 ・内容一致問題がほとんどだが、中には、文挿入問題や、表現の意図、語彙の意味を問うものもある。	

Unit 1 Daily Life

品詞

Goal

・TOEIC L&R で出題される日常的な場面設定の英文に慣れる
・TOEIC L&R 攻略の第一歩として品詞の基礎知識を身に付ける

 Warm-Up Questions DL 02 CD1-02

日本語訳を参考に、空所に入る語を (A) ～ (D) から選びましょう。

1. お手伝いくださりありがとうございます。

   Thank you for your -------.

   (A) helpfully　　(B) helpful　　(C) help　　(D) helped

2. 私たちは常にお客様のニーズを意識しています。

   We are always ------- of customer needs.

   (A) conscious　　(B) consciousness　　(C) consciously　　(D) conscience

 Words & Expressions DL 03 CD1-03

音声を聞いて、日本語訳に合う語を（　　）内に書き入れましょう。

1. 最高の時間　　　　　　　　　(q _ _ _ _ _ _) time
2. 理解のあるスタッフ　　　　　staff members who are (u _ _ _ _ _ _ _ _ _ _ _ _)
3. すばやい返信　　　　　　　　a quick (r _ _ _ _ _ _ _)
4. 商品の状態　　　　　　　　　the product (c _ _ _ _ _ _ _ _)
5. 壊れやすい品物　　　　　　　a (f _ _ _ _ _ _) item
6. 結婚式に出席する　　　　　　(a _ _ _ _ _) a wedding
7. 私の親戚の一人　　　　　　　one of my (r _ _ _ _ _ _ _ _)
8. よく計画されたリスト　　　　a (w _ _ _ - _ _ _ _ _ _ _) list
9. 慈善活動　　　　　　　　　　(c _ _ _ _ _ _ _ _ _) work
10. 着るものを選ぶ　　　　　　　(p _ _ _) what to wear
11. 目を覚ましている　　　　　　stay (a _ _ _ _)
12. 魅力的なマーケット　　　　　an (a _ _ _ _ _ _ _ _ _) market
13. 不動産の専門家　　　　　　　a real (e _ _ _ _ _) expert
14. 物件を見つける　　　　　　　find some (p _ _ _ _ _ _ _)
15. 関係を築く　　　　　　　　　build (r _ _ _ _ _ _ _ _ _ _ _ _)

Grammar Focus 品詞の基礎知識

英語を正確に理解するためには品詞の基礎的な知識が欠かせません。実際にTOEIC L&Rでも品詞の理解が問題を解く鍵になることは珍しくありません。全てをここで挙げることはできませんが、まずは最低限重要なものに絞って確認しておきましょう。

名　詞	人・物・事を表す
代名詞	名詞の代わりに用いる
動　詞	主語の動作や状態を表す
形容詞	名詞の状態や性質について説明を加える
副　詞	形容詞、動詞、文などについて説明を加える
前置詞	名詞の前に用いて、場所・方向・時間・関係性などを表す
接続詞	文同士、語句・表現同士をつなぐ

これらを念のため確認しておくことがTOEIC L&R 攻略への第一歩です。具体的には以下の問題を通して学んでいきましょう。

 **Practice**

空所に入る語を語群から選び、文を完成させましょう。選択肢は一度しか使えません。

1. The product condition was far from -------.
2. The smart speaker I bought yesterday was -------.
3. All of our staff members are -------.
4. It was raining ------- yesterday, so we stayed home.
5. Thank you ------- your quick response.
6. Would you mind ------- coming with you?
7. We help you ------- quality time with your family.
8. I was not informed ------- the event.
9. We should be careful when ------- fragile items.
10. It is our ------- to always keep track of expenses.

A. broken	**B.** perfect	**C.** responsibility	**D.** of	**E.** understanding
F. handling	**G.** me	**H.** for	**I.** spend	**J.** heavily

Short Listening 🎧 DL 05   ⊙ CD1-05

次の会話を聞いて、1 〜 4 の（　　　）に語を書き入れましょう。そのあと、5 と 6 の質問に日本語で答えましょう。

M: Hello, Emily. I'm going shopping (¹.　　　　) Tom's birthday party today. Can you come with me?

W: I have a dental appointment this morning, but I think I have (²　　　　　　　　) time in my schedule after that.

M: That's great (³.　　　) hear. Can (⁴.　　　) meet in front of the ticket gate at Brook Station at 1:00 P.M.?

W: Yes, of course.

---

5. 男性は今日、何のために買い物に行く予定ですか。

6. 2 人は何時にどこで集合しますか。

_____

 Short Reading 🎧 DL 06   ⊙ CD1-06

次の E メールを読んで、1 〜 3 の質問に日本語で答えましょう。

Hi Jessie,

It's been a long time. I haven't seen you since we met last year. How are you doing? Today, I'm writing this to let you know some good news. I'm going to Boston on the 10th of September to attend the wedding of one of my relatives. Since I am going to be near where you live, I would love to see you if you are available. I am looking forward to your reply.

Best,

Linda

---

1. リンダがジェシーに最後に会ったのはいつですか。

2. リンダがボストンに行く目的は何ですか。

3. リンダは何を望んでいますか。

_____

TOEIC Practice

Listening

> **Tips!** Part 1 の写真の大きな分類としては、人が写っているかどうかが重要です。人が写っている場合はその人（々）が何をしているのか、人が写っていない場合は情景全体や、ものの位置関係によく注目してください。Part 2 はまずは TOEIC L&R の応答問題の基本的な形式である、WH 疑問文の問題に慣れるつもりで取り組みましょう。

Part 1

CheckLink   DL 07   CD1-07

Look at the picture and select the statement that best describes what you see in the picture.

1.

(A) (B) (C) (D)

2.

(A) (B) (C) (D)

Part 2

CheckLink   DL 08   CD1-08

Listen to the question or statement and the three responses. Then select the best response to each question or statement.

1. (A)　　(B)　　(C)

2. (A)　　(B)　　(C)

3. (A)　　(B)　　(C)

Tips!> Part 5 では、品詞の意識が何よりも大切です。どの選択肢であれば文法的に空所に入ることができるのか、焦らずに丁寧に検討してみましょう。この意識は Part 6 でも同じです。最初はスピードにこだわらず、知識を総動員して考えてみましょう。

Part 5

CheckLink   DL 09   CD1-09

Select the best answer to complete the sentence.

1. ------- a movie at home is never complete without your favorite snacks.
   (A) Watch   (B) Watching   (C) Watches   (D) Watched

2. Making a well-planned grocery list ------- you go shopping is very important.
   (A) before   (B) in   (C) since   (D) during

3. Tarr's Kitchen serves a ------- breakfast at incredibly reasonable prices.
   (A) nutrition   (B) nutritious   (C) nutritiously   (D) nutriment

4. At Joe's Clothing Store, everyone can find clothes that suit them -------.
   (A) perfection   (B) perfects   (C) perfectly   (D) perfect

5. The bus always ------- two stops before Ms. Sanders gets to work.
   (A) makes   (B) maker   (C) make   (D) making

6. In ------- free time, Mr. Reed and his wife take part in volunteer activities.
   (A) their   (B) they   (C) them   (D) theirs

7. Henry's Furniture is known for its charitable -------.
   (A) worked   (B) workable   (C) workless   (D) work

8. The survey has revealed that many customers always have a ------- time picking what to wear.
   (A) hardly   (B) hard   (C) harden   (D) hardness

9. Ms. Jefferson stayed ------- until midnight thinking about the project she was involved in.
   (A) wake   (B) awaken   (C) awake   (D) woke

10. Membership at TG Gym will ------- you for the discount.
    (A) quality   (B) qualify   (C) be qualified   (D) qualitative

Part 6

CheckLink DL 10 CD1-10

Questions 1-4 refer to the following advertisement.

FIND YOUR DREAM HOME

To All Southside Residents,

The current housing market has never been so attractive for homebuyers, and our team of real estate experts is here to help you find your dream home. Prices are at a ten-year low, and banks are offering low rates to buyers. It's an ------- time to
1.
look into buying a house, and we at the Legacy Realtor Group want to help you find your next home. The agents at Legacy will work with you to understand your -------
2.
needs and find the property perfect for you specifically. -------, they have years of
3.
experience working in the field and have built relationships with contractors and landowners all across the city. They'll know the leads that other agents can't offer you. -------.
4.

The Legacy Realtor Group

---

1. (A) excited
(B) exciting
(C) excite
(D) excitedly

2. (A) unique
(B) approximate
(C) challenged
(D) threatening

3. (A) Furthermore
(B) Otherwise
(C) Although
(D) Therefore

4. (A) New tax benefits are available for new owners.
(B) Contact us to schedule a meeting with a Legacy agent today.
(C) Buying a home by yourself is easier than ever.
(D) We hope you'll join our team of expert agents.

Unit 2 Office

代名詞

Goal

・オフィスに関する基礎的な語彙・表現を身に付け、関連する英文を読む力を付ける

・代名詞の基礎的な使い方を再確認して、Part 5 の得点力を上げる

 ## Warm-Up Questions　　　　　　🎧 DL 11　　◎ CD1-11

日本語訳を参考に、空所に入る語を (A) ～ (D) から選びましょう。

1. 質問があれば 1100-2230 に遠慮なく電話してください。

Feel free to contact ------- at 1100-2230 with any questions.

(A) we　　　(B) our　　　(C) us　　　(D) ours

2. 全てのスタッフはこの新しいシステムに働いた時間を入力しなければいけません。

All the staff members should enter ------- work hours into this new system.

(A) they　　　(B) their　　　(C) them　　　(D) theirs

 ## Words & Expressions　　　　　🎧 DL 12　　◎ CD1-12

音声を聞いて、日本語訳に合う語を (　　) 内に書き入れましょう。

1. 秘書に連絡する　　　　　　　　contact the (s _ _ _ _ _ _ _ _)

2. 紙詰まり　　　　　　　　　　　a paper (j _ _)

3. クレームが来ると予想する　　　expect a (c _ _ _ _ _ _ _ _)

4. コピー機を新しいものに取り替える　(r _ _ _ _ _ _) the copier with a new one

5. 経理部　　　　　　　　　　　　the accounting (d _ _ _ _ _ _ _)

6. 技術者を必要とする　　　　　　need a (t _ _ _ _ _ _ _ _ _)

7. 貴重な感想　　　　　　　　　　(v _ _ _ _ _ _ _) feedback

8. 広範囲のマーケット調査をする　do (e _ _ _ _ _ _ _ _) market research

9. 快適なオフィス　　　　　　　　a (c _ _ _ _ _ _ _ _ _ _) office

10. 顧客に電話をする　　　　　　　(g _ _ _) the client a call

11. その機械を修理する　　　　　　(f _ _) the machine

12. 安心している　　　　　　　　　rest (a _ _ _ _ _ _)

13. 皆に感銘を与える　　　　　　　(i _ _ _ _ _ _) everyone

14. そのレストランの新しい場所　　the new (l _ _ _ _ _ _ _) of the restaurant

15. 開店に先立ち　　　　　　　　　in (a _ _ _ _ _ _) of the opening

Grammar Focus　　代名詞

代名詞は英語の基礎中の基礎です。英文の意味を正確に理解するには代名詞の理解は欠かせません。念のため、確認しておきましょう。

人称	数	人称代名詞			所有代名詞	再帰代名詞
		主格	目的格	所有格		
一人称	単数	I	me	my	mine	myself
	複数	we	us	our	ours	ourselves
二人称	単数	you	you	your	yours	yourself
	複数					yourselves
三人称	単数	he	him	his	his	himself
		she	her	her	hers	herself
		it	it	its	—	itself
	複数	they	them	their	theirs	themselves

 Practice　　DL 13　CD1-13

空所に入る語を語群から選び、文を完成させましょう。選択肢は一度しか使えません。

1. Given ------- background in the field of finance, I am qualified for this position.
2. Ms. Sato was congratulated on ------- achievement.
3. I will participate in ------- of the conferences.
4. As you might already know, ------- office is moving to a new location.
5. If you notice any changes, you should communicate ------- to your coworker.
6. Please note that ------- have decided to order a new copier.
7. The cabinet we released ten years ago is well known for ------- durability.
8. Your feedback is very valuable as ------- helps us improve our service.
9. Thank you for providing ------- with the sample of your work.
10. Let me introduce a colleague of -------.

A. we	**B.** both	**C.** our	**D.** mine	**E.** it
F. my	**G.** them	**H.** us	**I.** its	**J.** her

次の広告を聞いて、1 ～ 4 の（　　　）に語を書き入れましょう。そのあと、5 と 6 の質問に日本語で答えましょう。

W: Are you having trouble (¹·⎯⎯⎯⎯⎯⎯⎯⎯⎯) your office equipment? If so, don't hesitate to call us. We will send a (²·⎯⎯⎯⎯⎯⎯⎯⎯⎯) to help you right away. From large cabinets to desk (³·⎯⎯⎯⎯⎯⎯⎯⎯⎯), we can repair a wide range of products in no time. If there's (⁴·⎯⎯⎯⎯⎯⎯⎯⎯⎯) we can do to help, please let us know.

---

5. この会社は何の修理を扱っていますか。

_____

6. 話し手は、聞き手に何をすることをお願いしていますか。

_____

 **Short Reading**   DL 15   CD1-15

次のウェブサイトを読んで、1 ～ 3 の質問に日本語で答えましょう。

□　　　　　　　　　　　　　　　　　　　　　　　　　　　　　　　− □ ×

M & B OFFICE SERVICES

Would you like a comfortable office? It is important to set up an office quickly so that you can start operating immediately after starting your business.

We have been developing and selling office supplies for many years. In order to make our experience more useful to society, we have started a business where we send our staff to help you set up your office. From installing some nice ceiling lights to setting up your laptop, we can do it all. Please send any inquiries to inqury@mboffice.com.

---

1. オフィスの開設をすばやく済ませることはなぜ大切なのですか。

_____

2. M&B オフィスサービスはどのような業務経験がありますか。

_____

3. M&B オフィスサービスは読み手に何を求めていますか。

_____

TOEIC Practice

Listening

Tips! オフィスの場面設定の問題に挑戦します。Part 1 では写真全体に何が写っているかをよく確認しましょう。Part 3 は主に会社のどこで会話が行われているか、誰と誰が会話をしているのかなどを意識して聞くようにしましょう。

Part 1

 CheckLink   DL 16   CD1-16

Look at the picture and select the statement that best describes what you see in the picture.

1.

(A) (B) (C) (D)

2.

(A) (B) (C) (D)

Part 3

 CheckLink   DL 17   CD1-17

Listen to the conversation and select the best response to each question.

1. Where does this conversation take place?
   (A) In the CEO's office
   (B) In the General Affairs division
   (C) In the Accounting division
   (D) In the Sales division

2. What is the problem with copiers?
   (A) They need a new toner cartridge.
   (B) They are out of paper.
   (C) They have paper jams.
   (D) They have paper feeder problems.

3. What will the speakers probably do next?
   (A) They will order new copiers from the copier company.
   (B) They will sign a new lease with the copier company.
   (C) They will ask the copier company to replace all their copiers with new ones.
   (D) They will ask the copier company to send someone to check their machines.

Tips! 代名詞の理解はどのパートでも重要ですが、特に Part 5 では取りこぼさないようにしたいところです。基礎的なことが分かっていればすぐに解ける問題がほとんどなので、この Unit で攻略しておきましょう。Part 7 は場面をよく意識しながら、「正解を探す」のではなく、「英文を理解する」意識で臨んでください。

Part 5

 CheckLink DL 18 CD1-18

Select the best answer to complete the sentence.

1. The technician repaired the machine, and ------- now works fine.

    (A) they   (B) he   (C) it   (D) these

2. He attended the tradeshow on behalf of ------- company.

    (A) our   (B) us   (C) we   (D) ours

3. Ms. Page's laptop is broken, so she needs to buy a new -------.

    (A) it   (B) them   (C) one   (D) another

4. The employees must enter their work hours by -------.

    (A) them   (B) their   (C) theirs   (D) themselves

5. The marketing team has done extensive research, and they now need to submit reports about -------.

    (A) it   (B) those   (C) them   (D) one

6. ------- employee directory has not been updated.

    (A) We   (B) Us   (C) Ours   (D) Our

7. ------- who need reimbursement for travel expenses should talk to their supervisor.

    (A) Those   (B) One   (C) Anyone   (D) Each

8. Wheeler Tech's new software helps business owners manage ------- e-mails.

    (A) they   (B) their   (C) them   (D) theirs

9. We have received twenty portfolios with samples, and ------- was one of the top five.

    (A) you   (B) your   (C) yours   (D) yourself

10. The president invited some of his former colleagues to the party, and all of ------- were very glad.

    (A) them   (B) they   (C) theirs   (D) their

Part 7

CCheckLink 🎧 DL 19 ◉ CD1-19

Questions 1-3 refer to the following notice.

Upcoming Training Session

To: All Bennet Foods Employees
From: Sophia Bennet, CEO
Date: December 20

Since the closing of our Waffle House restaurant, we have been looking for something else to put at that location. Through a casual meeting at a tradeshow in July, we became acquainted with Chef Shira Feldman. Chef Feldman is extremely inventive. She catered the last executive board meeting, and everyone was impressed by her food, so we have decided to open a new restaurant with her.

As she specializes in Pacific fusion, we plan to call the new restaurant "Pacific Cuisine Shira." In order not to lose our shirts in this venture, we have done extensive market research. So those of you who work on the restaurant side can rest assured that we plan to make this a success.

On January 10, we plan to bring together all employees for special training. It will be a full day for restaurant staff, and until 1:00 P.M. for headquarters staff. Chef Feldman and my team will explain the new concept. She will then treat us to a tasty lunch. In the afternoon, restaurant staff will learn about the new menu and service standards in advance of the opening in March.

---

1. What is the purpose of the notice?
   (A) To announce the new location of the Waffle House restaurant
   (B) To outline corporate training with a new chef
   (C) To ask the recipient to evaluate the Waffle House restaurant
   (D) To launch a Pacific fusion cuisine recipe contest

2. Where did the CEO first meet Chef Feldman?
   (A) At a restaurant
   (B) At an industry show
   (C) At a board meeting
   (D) At a family gathering

3. What are restaurant workers required to do?
   (A) Think of menu ideas
   (B) Stay for afternoon training
   (C) Visit the company headquarters
   (D) Decide where they wish to work

Meeting & Event

前置詞と接続詞 1

Goal
- 会議やイベントに関する語彙・表現を身に付け、英文からそれらの情報を正確に読み取ることができる
- 同じような意味をもつ前置詞と接続詞の区別が理解できる

 ## Warm-Up Questions　🎧 DL 20　◎ CD1-20

日本語訳を参考に、空所に入る語を（A）～（D）から選びましょう。

1. 彼女はキャリアの中で 10 を超える映画を制作しました。

She created more than ten films ------- her career.

(A) since　　(B) for　　(C) while　　(D) during

2. 悪天候のためにフライトの予定が変更されました。

The flight schedule was changed ------- inclement weather.

(A) despite　　(B) due to　　(C) since　　(D) because

 ## Words & Expressions　🎧 DL 21　◎ CD1-21

音声を聞いて、日本語訳に合う語を（　　）内に書き入れましょう。

1. 精神面での利点　　　　　　　psychological (**b** _ _ _ _ _ _ _)

2. 年に一度のワークショップ　　an (**a** _ _ _ _ _) workshop

3. 前向きな態度　　　　　　　　a positive (**a** _ _ _ _ _ _ _)

4. セミナー受講料　　　　　　　the seminar (**f** _ _)

5. 席を 4 月 2 日までに予約する　(**r** _ _ _ _ _ _) a seat by April 2

6. 締め切りまでに　　　　　　　by the (**d** _ _ _ _ _ _ _)

7. 新入社員説明会　　　　　　　an (**o** _ _ _ _ _ _ _ _ _ _) for new employees

8. 会社の目的　　　　　　　　　the company's (**o** _ _ _ _ _ _ _ _ _)

9. プロジェクトについて議論する　discuss a (**p** _ _ _ _ _ _)

10. それぞれの部署の業務　　　　the (**r** _ _ _ _ _ _ _ _ _ _ _ _ _ _ _) of each division

11. 前もって　　　　　　　　　　(**a** _ _ _ _) of time

12. 同僚に会う　　　　　　　　　meet a (**c** _ _ _ _ _ _ _)

13. 会社の最近のプロジェクト　　recent (**c** _ _ _ _ _ _ _ _) projects

14. 遠慮せずに私にメールしてください。Feel (**f** _ _ _) to e-mail me.

15. あなたの写真付き身分証明書を　(**P** _ _ _ _ _ _) your photo ID.
　　　提示してください。

Grammar Focus　　前置詞と接続詞の違い

Part 5 では似たような意味をもつ前置詞と接続詞がよく問われます。前置詞の後ろには名詞相当語句が、接続詞の後ろには文が来るのが基本です。

意味	前置詞	接続詞
〜にもかかわらず	in spite of / despite	although / though / while / even if / even though
〜の間	for / during	while
〜なので	because of / due to / thanks to / owing to / on account of	because / as / since
〜の場合に	in case of / in the event of	in case (that) / in the event (that)
〜まで	by（期限） until（継続）	by the time（期限） until（継続）
〜を除いて	except (for) / but / aside from	except that / but that
〜のあとで	following / after / subsequent to	after
〜の前に	before / prior to	before

※ ただし、一部の接続詞では、主語 + be 動詞が省略され、結果的に接続詞の後ろに分詞などが続く形になるものもあります。

Practice　　　　　　　　　 DL 22　　 CD1-22

空所に入る語句を語群から選び、文を完成させましょう。選択肢は一度しか使えません。なお、文頭に来る語も小文字で与えられています。

1. Please enter the information ------- the form closes.
2. You need to fill in the form ------- the opening of the session.
3. I was very happy with the accommodation ------- my stay in San Francisco.
4. We need to change the venue ------- some roadwork.
5. I decided to attend the seminar ------- the fee.
6. We have been working on a new project ------- the last meeting.
7. We are not able to give you a refund ------- the deadline was yesterday.
8. Please keep all your valuables with you ------- you are away from your seat.
9. ------- we are a small business, we are highly acclaimed in this industry.
10. Please remain seated ------- the intermission.

A. although	**B.** prior to	**C.** while	**D.** since	**E.** during
F. because	**G.** before	**H.** despite	**I.** until	**J.** because of

🔷 Short Listening

🎧 DL 23　◎ CD1-23

次の会話を聞いて、1 〜 4 の（　　）に語を書き入れましょう。そのあと、5 と 6 の質問に日本語で答えましょう。

W: Have you been (1.　　　　　　　　) of the annual training workshop?
M: Yes, and I (2.　　　　　　　) the person in charge to apply.
W: Then, did you receive a (3.　　　　　　　　) e-mail?
M: Yes, I got one shortly (4.　　　　　　) I sent my e-mail.
W: That's good to hear. I'm going to attend the workshop as well.
M: Great. I'm really looking forward to it.

5. 年に 1 回、何が開催されますか。

6. 男性はいつ確認メールを受け取りましたか。

🔷 Short Reading

🎧 DL 24　◎ CD1-24

次の手紙を読んで、1 〜 3 の質問に日本語で答えましょう。

Dear new employees,

We provide training for new employees who have started working at the head office. During the training, you will receive lectures from experienced employees on how to deal with customers, handle complaints, and perform various administrative tasks. Participation in the training is mandatory. The venue is a conference room on the second floor of the headquarters building. When you arrive that day, please present your photo ID to the receptionist. The receptionist will show you to your seat.

1. 研修では何を学びますか。

2. 研修の会場はどこですか。

3. 参加者は何を提示しないといけませんか。

TOEIC Practice

Listening

> **Tips!** TOEIC L&R の Part 2 はとにかく設問文を正確によく聞き取ることが大切です。この Unit では否定を含んだものを練習しましょう。Part 4 は選択肢を見ずに、設問だけ先に見て、どのような情報を聞き取りたいのかを意識した上で本文を聞きましょう。

Part 2

Listen to the question or statement and the three responses. Then select the best response to each question or statement.

1. (A)   (B)   (C)
2. (A)   (B)   (C)
3. (A)   (B)   (C)

Part 4

Listen to the talk and select the best response to each question.

1. What does the speaker imply when he says, "We've got something for you"?
  (A) His company will hire some more staff.
  (B) He has an answer for the problem.
  (C) Most people have to be ready for the change.
  (D) He bought some presents for the listeners.

2. What is mentioned as part of this seminar?
  (A) Brainstorming
  (B) Some lecturing
  (C) A book signing
  (D) Musical exercises

3. What should an interested person do?
  (A) Send an e-mail to the radio station
  (B) Make a booking by phone by the deadline
  (C) Just go to Carpenter Hall on July 27
  (D) Get a copy of the doctor's book

Reading

Tips! Part 5 では前置詞と接続詞の基本的な問題を解く練習をします。これまでに学習したこと
をよく思い出しながら、知識が自分のものになっているか確認してください。Part 6 は研
修に関する英文を読みます。Part 7 と同様に、問題を解くことよりもまず、英文そのもの
をよく理解することを意識して取り組んでみましょう。

Part 5

CheckLink　🎧 DL 27　◎ CD1-27

Select the best answer to complete the sentence.

1. That employee has come up with a great idea ------- the workshop.
   (A) to　　(B) among　　(C) as　　(D) for

2. We regret to inform you that the conference has been postponed ------- November.
   (A) until　　(B) on　　(C) when　　(D) at

3. The Planning Department needs to reschedule the event ------- March 3.
   (A) with　　(B) in　　(C) for　　(D) during

4. The participants in the conference will be served complimentary refreshments -------
   the break.
   (A) while　　(B) during　　(C) up　　(D) in case

5. Ms. Lewis gained a lot of knowledge of this field ------- she was speaking with her
   coworkers.
   (A) during　　(B) in　　(C) while　　(D) on

6. Please make sure to fill in the questionnaire shortly ------- the event.
   (A) after　　(B) when　　(C) while　　(D) by

7. Please write down your name on the sheet ------- we need to confirm the participants.
   (A) to　　(B) due to　　(C) by　　(D) because

8. The seminar was canceled ------- terrible weather conditions.
   (A) at　　(B) because　　(C) due to　　(D) of

9. Employees must submit a report to their supervisor ------- the orientation.
   (A) by the time　　(B) because　　(C) when　　(D) after

10. Please sign up online to join the event scheduled ------- January 5.
    (A) with　　(B) to　　(C) for　　(D) in

Part 6

Questions 1-4 refer to the following e-mail.

From: Jeannie Nelson

To: Brian Lee

Subject: Orientation packet

Date: August 30

Attachment: A Guide to Orientation

Dear Brian,

------- our entire staff, I would like to welcome you to Maywood Innovative IT Solutions.
  1.

You are scheduled for the one-week new employee orientation that begins on

September 13. Attached is a file entitled "A Guide to Orientation." This file provides

overall information about the company, and it includes an explanation of the

company's core values and objectives. Your orientation will be ------- based on this
                                             2.

information, so you need to read it over ahead of time for a full understanding of the

content. At the orientation we will discuss recent corporate projects and achievements.

-------, you will be introduced to several of your coworkers so you can get a feel for
  3.

the responsibilities of each division. -------.
                                   4.

Regards,

Jeannie Nelson

Manager, Human Resources

---

1. (A) On behalf of
   (B) In exchange for
   (C) For the sake of
   (D) In honor of

2. (A) predicted
   (B) glimpsed
   (C) conducted
   (D) delayed

3. (A) Otherwise
   (B) Meanwhile
   (C) Moreover
   (D) Nevertheless

4. (A) The CEO attended the orientation last year.
   (B) I'm writing this in response to your inquiry.
   (C) They were happy to meet you at the orientation.
   (D) If you have any questions, please feel free to e-mail me.

Shopping

前置詞と接続詞 2

Goal

・TOEIC L&R に頻出の買い物に関する必須語彙・表現を学習し、関連する英文をすばやく読めるようになる
・前置詞と接続詞のやや発展的な頻出事項を整理し、慣用表現を身に付ける

▣ **Warm-Up Questions**   🎧 DL 29   CD1-29

日本語訳を参考に、空所に入る語を (A) ～ (D) から選びましょう。

1. あなたが倉庫に到着したら、すぐに私に連絡してください。

   Please contact me ------- you arrive at the warehouse.

   (A) as soon as   (B) on   (C) shortly   (D) then

2. 私たちは商品を返品できるように、再びその店に行きました。

   We visited the store again in order ------- we could return the product.

   (A) that   (B) to   (C) for   (D) of

▣ **Words & Expressions**   🎧 DL 30 ◎ CD1-30

音声を聞いて、日本語訳に合う語を (   ) 内に書き入れましょう。

1. パーティーを主催する   (**h** _ _ _) a party
2. 在庫一掃セール   a (**c** _ _ _ _ _ _ _ _) sale
3. 発送の手配をする   arrange for (**s** _ _ _ _ _ _ _)
4. 客にすぐに連絡する   contact the customer (**i** _ _ _ _ _ _ _ _ _ _)
5. 結局遅れて到着する   (**e** _ _) up arriving late
6. 問題を解決する   (**f** _ _) a problem
7. その会社への連絡を試みる   (**r** _ _ _ _) out to the company
8. 豪華な景品   (**g** _ _ _ _ _ _ _) prizes
9. 10 ドルの取扱手数料   a $10 (**h** _ _ _ _ _ _ _) charge
10. 商品を翌日配送する   deliver the item (**o** _ _ _ _ _ _ _ _)
11. 喜びを分かち合う機会   an (**o** _ _ _ _ _ _ _ _ _ _) to share the joys
12. クーポンを同封する   (**i** _ _ _ _ _ _) a coupon
13. 損失を補償する   (**c** _ _ _ _ _ _ _ _ _) for loss
14. 最大参加人数   the (**m** _ _ _ _ _ _) number of participants
15. 大変な迷惑をかける   cause great (**i** _ _ _ _ _ _ _ _ _ _ _ _)

Grammar Focus　　前置詞と接続詞の重要表現

ここではさらに発展的な事項について整理しておきましょう。TOEIC L&R では単に前置詞と接続詞の区別がつくかだけでなく、慣用的な表現を知っているかどうかも問われます。特によく出るものを以下にまとめます。

前置詞を使った重要表現		接続詞を使った重要表現	
without -ing	～せずに	so that SV	S が V するために、S が V するように
into	～まで（続いて）	in order that SV	S が V するために
in[with] regard to	～に関して	in that SV	S が V なので、S が V の点で
regardless of	～にかかわらず	provided that SV	S が V という条件で
notwithstanding	～にもかかわらず	as long as SV	S が V という条件で（S が V する限り）
along with	～とともに	as soon as SV	S が V するとすぐに
on -ing [名詞]	～の直後に	unless SV	S が V でない限り
beyond one's understanding	理解できない	not only A but also B	A だけでなく B も
from A through B	A から B まで（期間）	whether or not SV	S が V するかどうか
A as well as B	A と B、B と同様 A		

 Practice　　 DL 31　　 CD1-31

空所に入る語句を語群から選び、文を完成させましょう。選択肢は一度しか使えません。

1. I'd be glad to go shopping with you, ------- I have finished my work.
2. Our store is open from Monday ------- Friday.
3. The online sale continued deep ------- the night.
4. Statistics have indicated ------- most of our customers were satisfied.
5. Please come to the information desk ------- your arrival.
6. Did you experience any inconvenience ------- this issue?
7. You will receive a coupon ------- a free sample of our product.
8. Please give us your feedback ------- we can use it to assess and improve our service.
9. Some parts of the instruction manual were ------- my understanding.
10. The event at the shopping complex will be postponed ------- some additional people apply.

A. in regard to	**B.** on	**C.** so that	**D.** through	**E.** beyond
F. along with	**G.** unless	**H.** into	**I.** provided that	**J.** that

 **Short Listening**

次のアナウンスを聞いて、1〜4の（　　）に語を書き入れましょう。そのあと、5と6の質問に日本語で答えましょう。

> **M:** Hello, shoppers! I (¹.   ) you are enjoying your shopping today. We will be having a women's clothing (².   ) sale at the event space on the second floor from 1:00 P.M. today. The sale is (³.   ) to end at 5:00 P.M. but may finish earlier if everything is sold out. Some items will be 50% off the original (⁴.   ), so don't miss this opportunity. Please come by and take a look.

5. このアナウンスはどこで流れている可能性が高いですか。

_____

6. 今日の午後1時から、2階で何が行われますか。

_____

 Short Reading

次のお知らせを読んで、1〜3の質問に日本語で答えましょう。

> ### Evergreen Hills Mall Lottery
>
> On October 25 at 3:00 P.M., there will be a drawing for children at the toy corner on the 4th floor. Why not join in the fun with your children? We will be waiting for you with gorgeous prizes. Of course, all participants will receive a gift. The maximum number of participants is 50, and the event will be closed on a first-come, first-served basis. If you want to participate, please come early.

1. 10月25日の午後3時から、4階で何が行われますか。

_____

2. プレゼントをもらえるのは誰ですか。

_____

3. 参加するためには何をすることが必要ですか。

_____

TOEIC Practice

Listening

Tips! Part 2 では平叙文に対して平叙文で応答するやりとりが多く出題されます。場面をよく想像して適切なものを選びましょう。Part 3 は会話の全体像をおさえつつ、細部の情報も聞き取ることを意識してください。

Part 2

Listen to the question or statement and the three responses. Then select the best response to each question or statement.

1. (A)   (B)   (C)
2. (A)   (B)   (C)
3. (A)   (B)   (C)

Part 3

Listen to the conversation and select the best response to each question.

1. What is the conversation mainly about?
   (A) A snack bar in the break room
   (B) A store opening soon in the area
   (C) A visit to the company's warehouse
   (D) An upcoming party at the office

2. What do the men imply about POW?
   (A) It is hard to get there from their office.
   (B) It is likely a good place for them to shop.
   (C) It is where they should look for some snacks.
   (D) It might be hard for them to get a discount.

3. Why does the woman say, "I'm available tonight"?
   (A) To agree to the shopping trip
   (B) To arrange a private dinner
   (C) To attend the dinner party
   (D) To confirm the party is on May 7

Tips! Part 5 では、空所の後ろにどの品詞が来るのかを丁寧に確認し、前置詞と接続詞のどちらが入るかを判断しましょう。Part 7 では、自分がその英文の当事者になったつもりで読んでみましょう。

Part 5

CheckLink DL 36 CD1-36

Select the best answer to complete the sentence.

1. A sales representative will get back to you ------- the item is ready for shipping.
   (A) as soon as　　(B) that　　(C) then　　(D) on

2. Ms. Grubb described the situation clearly ------- the person in charge could locate the problem.
   (A) along with　　(B) because of　　(C) in order that　　(D) in regard to

3. Fineware's products include traditional Asian tableware ------- Western tableware.
   (A) along　　(B) as well as　　(C) in regard to　　(D) provided that

4. We are fortunate ------- we have a lot of loyal customers like you.
   (A) with　　(B) because of　　(C) in that　　(D) then

5. Customers can place an order online ------- having to come to the store.
   (A) so that　　(B) not to　　(C) as　　(D) without

6. Please enjoy not only shopping but ------- a couple of events held in the store.
   (A) also about　　(B) also　　(C) as　　(D) in addition to

7. We will remove the item from layaway ------- the expired deadline.
   (A) regardless　　(B) because of　　(C) however　　(D) unless

8. Mr. Lee has not yet decided whether or not ------- a new vacuum cleaner.
   (A) about purchasing　　　　(C) purchase
   (B) purchasing　　　　　　(D) he will purchase

9. ------- its reasonable price, the scanner performs incredibly.
   (A) Since　　(B) Regardless　　(C) Notwithstanding　　(D) However

10. ------- this bad weather continues, we won't be able to go to the flea market.
    (A) Then　　(B) As long as　　(C) With　　(D) Even

Part 7

CheckLink DL 37 · CD1-37

Questions 1-5 refer to the following e-mails.

To: customerservice@polarice.com
From: fredrico.d@starmail.com
Date: January 20
Subject: Broken Ice Maker

Hello,

A few days ago I received a Pellet Ice Maker that I ordered from your Web site. I was excited to see it since it arrived earlier than I expected, and I planned to use it for a party I was hosting. When I opened the box, however, there was a large crack along the front panel of the machine. The box did not appear damaged, so I don't think it was broken during shipping.

I plugged the ice maker in to see if it still worked. Unfortunately, the machine immediately started leaking water. I didn't see if it actually made ice, since I was worried the water might start an electrical fire. I ended up having to buy ice for the party instead since there wasn't enough time to order a new one. Is there any way you can fix this issue?

Fredrico Diaz

To: fredrico.d@starmail.com
From: customerservice@polarice.com
Date: January 21
Subject: Re: Broken Ice Maker

Dear Mr. Diaz,

Thank you for reaching out to us. We are sorry the Pellet Ice Maker you ordered from us did not reach the level of quality you should expect from us. We performed an investigation and realized the unit was damaged during handling at our warehouse. The shipping company who delivered it is not at fault, so we are thankful you contacted us directly.

We will be sending a new ice maker to you right away. This one will be triple-checked for defects and will be shipped overnight to you. We realize this does not fix the problem of its not being there for your party but hope you have the opportunity to use it more in the future. We will also be including a gift card to use for future purchases from our Web site. We hope this compensates for the inconvenience we caused.

Sincerely,

Polar Ice Customer Support

1. Why was Mr. Diaz excited to get the ice maker early?
   (A) He needed to use a gift card before it expired.
   (B) He needed to replace his old ice maker.
   (C) He was planning on using it for an event.
   (D) He wanted to test it before installing it.

2. Why didn't Mr. Diaz try to make any ice?
   (A) The shipment didn't have the necessary filter.
   (B) He had already had his party by the time it came.
   (C) The machine didn't come with instructions.
   (D) He was concerned about creating a danger.

3. What does the company say they will do to make sure the replacement works?
   (A) They will use a repaired machine.
   (B) They will investigate the box for damage.
   (C) They will check it multiple times.
   (D) They will send the latest version.

4. What does Polar Ice offer Mr. Diaz to make up for the mistake?
   (A) A voucher at their e-store
   (B) Free filters for the new machine
   (C) An upgraded ice machine
   (D) A coupon for shipping

5. What do Mr. Diaz and the company both agree on?
   (A) The shipping company isn't responsible for the damage.
   (B) An ice machine is necessary to hold a party.
   (C) Giving Mr. Diaz a replacement is enough to solve the issue.
   (D) The first ice machine did not arrive in time for the party.

Unit 5 Advertisement & Notice

助動詞

Goal

・TOEIC L&R に頻出の広告や告知に関する英文に触れ、重要語彙・表現を身に付ける
・助動詞の頻出問題をすばやく解けるように、知識を再確認する

 ## Warm-Up Questions　 DL 38　CD1-38

日本語訳を参考に、空所に入る語を (A) ～ (D) から選びましょう。

1. あなたは午後5時にそこにいるべきだったのに。

   You ------- have been there at 5 P.M.

   (A) must　　(B) should　　(C) would　　(D) will

2. その書類はすぐにあなたのところに届きます。

   The document ------- be sent to you immediately.

   (A) must　　(B) can　　(C) will　　(D) has to

Words & Expressions　DL 39　CD1-39

音声を聞いて、日本語訳に合う語を（　　）内に書き入れましょう。

1. 素晴らしい食事の経験　　　　a great (c _ _ _ _ _ _ _) experience
2. 工事中で　　　　　　　　　under (c _ _ _ _ _ _ _ _ _ _ _)
3. 出席の登録をする　　　　　(r _ _ _ _ _ _ _) to attend
4. 改装工事中で　　　　　　　under (r _ _ _ _ _ _ _ _ _)
5. 総務課　　　　　　　　　　the General Affairs (D _ _ _ _ _ _ _ _ _)
6. 提案する　　　　　　　　　(o _ _ _ _) suggestions
7. サンプルを配布する　　　　(p _ _ _) around samples
8. それを確かめる　　　　　　(c _ _ _ _) it out
9. 寄付を求める　　　　　　　request (d _ _ _ _ _ _ _ _)
10. 本のサイン会　　　　　　　a book (s _ _ _ _ _ _)
11. イベントを行う　　　　　　(c _ _ _ _) out an event
12. Tシャツが入手できる。　　T-shirts are (a _ _ _ _ _ _ _ _).
13. フェアの間ずっと　　　　　(t _ _ _ _ _ _ _ _ _) the fair
14. 地元の本屋　　　　　　　　(l _ _ _ _) bookstores
15. 立ち寄って参加する　　　　(c _ _ _) by to join in

39

Grammar Focus　助動詞

TOEIC L&Rでは助動詞の意味の違いが文法問題として直接問われることはまれです。とはいえ、学習しなくてよいというわけではありません。リスニングやリーディングには助動詞の理解は欠かせません。ここでは特に重要なものに絞って確認しましょう。

助動詞	意味
can	可能性、能力、許可、（Can you ...? で）依頼、（否定文で）禁止
could	can の過去形
may	推量、可能性、許可、提案
might	may の過去形。推量の意味で may と互換可能
must	義務、確信に近い推量、（否定文で）禁止
should（※ shall の過去形だが、実質現在形の独立した助動詞のようなもの）	義務、推量、（否定文で）禁止、提案・忠告
will	未来、話し手の意志、強い予測、（Will you ...? で）強い依頼
would	will の過去形、依頼・勧誘、（仮定法で）推量、婉曲

◎ やや発展的ですが、以下の表現も大切です。

　　would have ＋過去分詞：〜しただろうに　　must have ＋過去分詞：〜したに違いない

　　could have ＋過去分詞：〜した可能性がある　might have ＋過去分詞：〜したかもしれない

その他の助動詞（あるいは助動詞に相当する使い方をする表現）については問題演習で確認しましょう。

 # Practice　　　　　　　　　 DL 40　　 CD1-40

空所に入る語句を語群から選び、文を完成させましょう。選択肢は一度しか使えません。

1. The main street is currently under construction; you will ------- take a detour.
2. According to the weather forecast, it is ------- to snow tomorrow.
3. The door of the conference room ------- open, but now it functions properly.
4. If you ------- like to make a reservation, click the link below to fill in the form.
5. Everyone thought there was no way the CEO's resignation ------- be true.
6. Thanks to their aggressive promotional activities, the publisher ------- sell over a million copies of the novel.
7. You ------- register now to attend the workshop as the capacity is limited.
8. If by any chance you ------- make it to the event, please let us know before it starts.
9. The road ------- be too busy at this time of the day, so the TV crew should be here on time.
10. You ------- definitely enjoy a great culinary experience.

A. was able to	B. will	C. can't	D. going	E. would
F. shouldn't	G. wouldn't	H. should	I. have to	J. could

 **Short Listening**   🎧 DL 41   ◎ CD1-41

次の会話を聞いて、1 〜 4 の（　　）に語を書き入れましょう。そのあと、5 と 6 の質問に日本語で答えましょう。

M: Have you seen the (¹·   ) for the closing sale
     that's going on at H&R department store right now?

W: What? Are (²·   ) going to close? How long will the sale be going on?

M: I think (³·   ) end tomorrow. Most of the items have been discounted by
     up to 30%. (⁴·   ) better check it out right away.

W: Thanks! I'll stop by on my way home.

---

5. H&R デパートではなぜセールをしていますか。

6. 女性は帰宅前に何をするつもりですか。

 **Short Reading**   🎧 DL 42   ◎ CD1-42

次のお知らせを読んで、1 〜 3 の質問に日本語で答えましょう。

Renovation of Building 2

Dear employees,

As you already know, Building 2 will be under renovation from April 10 to
May 20. As a result, the parking lot in front of it will not be available during
the construction period. Employees who park their cars there should use the
parking lot next to Building 3. Could you please fill out the Parking Permit
Application Form and submit it to the General Affairs Department via e-mail?
Thank you for your patience.

---

1. この通知は誰に向けられたものですか。

2. 2 号館の改装工事の影響は何ですか。

3. 3 号館の隣の駐車場を使うには何をする必要がありますか。

Listening   Part 2, 4

Tips! Part 2 では疑問文に対して間接的な言い方で応答するやりとりがよく出題されます。答えを予測するのではなく、あくまでもその会話として自然なやりとりになるものを選ぶことが大切です。Part 4 は広告などもよく出題されます。短い時間でいろいろな情報が列挙されることがあるので、慣れが必要です。

Part 2   CheckLink DL 43 CD1-43

Listen to the question or statement and the three responses. Then select the best response to each question or statement.

1. (A)   (B)   (C)
2. (A)   (B)   (C)
3. (A)   (B)   (C)

Part 4   CheckLink DL 44 CD1-44

Listen to the talk and select the best response to each question.

1. Who is the woman most likely addressing?
   (A) A group of fitness experts
   (B) Members of her own staff
   (C) Mr. Macintosh and her staff
   (D) People trying to lose weight

2. What does the woman mean when she says, "Check it out for yourself"?
   (A) Buy the product at a store's self-checkout
   (B) Find out if you actually need the product
   (C) Research the supplement online later
   (D) Try actually taking the product

3. What does the woman imply her team will do?
   (A) Contact Mr. Macintosh to get some more samples
   (B) Discuss the supplement next time they get together
   (C) Do more research on the nutritional content of the supplement
   (D) Invite Mr. Macintosh to talk about product promotion

Reading

Tips! Part 5 では、文脈をよく見てどの選択肢であれば意味が最も自然かということと、文法的に可能なものはどれかということを同時に考えるようにしてください。Part 6 では、広告の文書を扱います。書き手が伝えたいことが伝わるようにするにはどのような文章の流れにするべきかを考えながら解答しましょう。

Part 5

CheckLink DL 45 CD1-45

Select the best answer to complete the sentence.

1. The gym offers customized service, and many of the members say they ------- more satisfied.

   (A) couldn't be   (B) had to   (C) must have been   (D) should have been

2. With the dynamic ads that the advertising agency creates, the clients ------- target prospective customers with pinpoint accuracy.

   (A) had to   (B) should have   (C) can   (D) must have

3. The consultant says the cosmetic firm ------- need to try newspaper ads in addition to digital ones.

   (A) may   (B) can   (C) have to   (D) must

4. The retailer ------- to move beyond traditional advertising channels to reach a wider audience.

   (A) will   (B) should   (C) must   (D) needs

5. The job announcement says that applicants ------- have at least three years of experience as a full-time teacher in order to be qualified.

   (A) used to   (B) must   (C) ought   (D) can

6. Starting tomorrow, there ------- be some roadwork on Sky Avenue, and commuters will have to take a detour.

   (A) will   (B) could   (C) can   (D) would

7. Behavioral targeting ------- be the key to the success of the start-up enterprise.

   (A) need   (B) ought   (C) might have   (D) could

8. It is imperative that every employee ------- streamline the process.

   (A) will   (B) should   (C) would   (D) could

9. This state-of-the-art dishwasher ------- surely reduce the burden of housework.

   (A) will   (B) need   (C) might   (D) able to

10. If you, by any chance, have trouble installing the software, you ------- contact the Engineering Department.

   (A) would often   (B) should   (C) had to   (D) used to

Questions 1-4 refer to the following advertisement.

Second Annual Community Book Fair

Come join us for our second annual book fair, coming Memorial Day Weekend at the community college campus! The fair is free to attend! And -------, you can get
1.
samples of new books coming out this summer.

Donations are requested and will benefit the local library system, but if you -------
2.
purchase something, all poster and T-shirt sales will fund the library as well.

Express your love of literature with other book lovers of all ages during this three-day event. -------. Local parchment maker Pergamos will be ------- an ancient
3.   **4.**
paper making process.

Book signings by Ori Dhyne and other prominent authors will be carried out throughout the fair. We will also be having children's book readings and performances as well. Come by to join in all the literary fun!

---

1. (A) even so
(B) what's more
(C) in spite of
(D) therefore

2. (A) stand by
(B) may well
(C) take on
(D) would rather

3. (A) Copies of his books for a book signing will be for sale.
(B) T-shirts are available in men's and women's sizes.
(C) Local bookstores will sell used and new books.
(D) We're being hosted by the college for the third year in a row.

4. (A) prolonging
(B) inspiring
(C) accepting
(D) demonstrating

Restaurant & Food

進行形と完了形

Goal

・ TOEIC L&R に頻出のレストランや食事の場面設定に慣れ、関連する英文を読めるようになる
・ 進行形と完了形の基本を整理し、時制による意味の違いを理解する

 ## Warm-Up Questions 🎧 DL 47 ⊙ CD2-02

日本語訳を参考に、空所に入る語を（A）～（D）から選びましょう。

1. レストランのドアに作業が施されているところです。

The door of the restaurant ------- on.

(A) is worked   (B) is being worked   (C) is working   (D) works

2. 皿がテーブルの上に並べられてあります。

Dishes ------- on the table.

(A) arranged   (C) have been arranged

(B) are being arranged   (D) are arranging

Words & Expressions 🎧 DL 48 ⊙ CD2-03

音声を聞いて、日本語訳に合う語を（　　）内に書き入れましょう。

1. 最も著名な批評家たち　　　　　the most (**d** _ _ _ _ _ _ _ _ _ _ _ _) critics

2. 接客産業　　　　　　　　　　　the (**h** _ _ _ _ _ _ _ _ _ _) industry

3. 食事券　　　　　　　　　　　　a (**m** _ _ _) coupon

4. 最大三人まで　　　　　　　　　(**u** _) to three people

5. 彼女の予約をキャンセルする　　cancel her (**r** _ _ _ _ _ _ _ _ _ _)

6. 彼女を他の日の予定に入れる　　(**r** _ _ _ _ _ _ _ _ _) her for another date

7. 宴会に参加する　　　　　　　　attend a (**b** _ _ _ _ _ _)

8. 客を惹きつける　　　　　　　　(**a** _ _ _ _ _ _) guests

9. 大皿料理を提供する　　　　　　provide (**p** _ _ _ _ _ _ _)

10. 通常の見積もり　　　　　　　　the usual (**e** _ _ _ _ _ _ _)

11. 追加料金　　　　　　　　　　　an (**a** _ _ _ _ _ _ _ _ _) fee

12. そのレストランをひいきにする　(**p** _ _ _ _ _ _ _ _) the restaurant

13. 当レストランの主力メニュー　　the (**f** _ _ _ _ _ _ _) item of our restaurant menu

14. デザートに対する割増料金　　　a (**s** _ _ _ _ _ _ _ _) for desserts

15. その問題を調べる　　　　　　　(**l** _ _ _) into the matter

Grammar Focus　　進行形と完了形

進行形と完了形は TOEIC L&R でよく出題されます。まずは基本となる頻出の形を確認し、それぞれの意味を考えてみましょう。

現在形	現在進行形
I **work** for a restaurant.	What **is** John **doing**? — He's **cooking** dinner.
現在完了形	現在完了進行形
Have you ever **been** to the dinner show?	How long **have** you **been studying** nutrition?
過去形	過去進行形
The doughnut shop **opened** last year.	We **weren't dining** out then.
過去完了形	過去完了進行形
I **had** already **visited** the café, so I knew that it was a good place.	I **had been working** on the new recipe for almost a year when my boss informed me of my promotion.
未来	未来進行形
We **will make** concerted efforts to produce better dishes than ever.	Ms. Griffith **will be joining** the dinner party.

なお、進行形と完了形の意味の違いを覚えておくと、Part 1 の問題に取り組む際に役に立ちます。ものが写っていて、それに対して人が何かの動作を行っているときは人を主語にした現在進行形や、ものを主語にした受け身の現在進行形が、人が不在でものに焦点が当たっていて、そのものの状態のみを表しているときは、ものを主語にした受け身の現在完了形がよく用いられます。

 # Practice DL 49　 CD2-04

空所に入る語句を語群から選び、文を完成させましょう。選択肢は一度しか使えません。

1. We ------- a dinner party on the fourth floor right now.

2. Ms. Kumar will join the culinary team after she ------- her current project.

3. She ------- one of the most distinguished Chinese food critics.

4. The opening of our new restaurant -------.

5. The chef ------- the new menu for two years before the opening.

6. The accounting staff ------- making the materials for three hours.

7. I hope you ------- your best dining experience ever.

8. Some dishes are still ------- cooked.

9. The restaurant ------- the Best Hospitality Award three times.

10. Every one of us ------- make our guests happy.

A. is always trying to	**B.** has finished	**C.** has been announced
D. has received	**E.** had worked on	**F.** are having
G. has been	**H.** have enjoyed	**I.** have been　　**J.** being

 ## Short Listening 🎧 DL 50 ⊙ CD2-05

次のアナウンスを聞いて、1〜4の（　）に語を書き入れましょう。そのあと、5と6の質問に日本語で答えましょう。

> **W:** Due to bad weather, the departure of this plane has been (¹·　　　　)
> for five hours. We apologize for any (²·　　　　) that this
> change in schedule (³·　　) cause. If you have a ticket for this flight,
> please come to the counter near Gate 7 to receive a free (⁴·　　) coupon.
> You can use it at any restaurant or café in this terminal. Thank you for your
> patience.

5. このアナウンスはどこで流れている可能性が高いですか。

_____

6. 7番ゲート近くのカウンターでは何がもらえますか。

_____

 ## Short Reading 🎧 DL 51 ⊙ CD2-06

次のお知らせを読んで、1〜3の質問に日本語で答えましょう。

AWESOME KITCHENWARE

  GET 20% OFF

AK52349

Thank you for always shopping with us. Today, we are happy to offer our loyal customers this special coupon so that you can enjoy our highest quality kitchen products at reasonable prices. To redeem this special coupon, fill in the coupon number on the code entry form on our Web site. After filling out the form, you will receive a 20 percent discount for all eligible items. The discount by coupon code can be applied to up to three products per customer.

1. この店は何を販売していますか。

_____

2. ウェブサイトには何が掲載されていますか。

_____

3. クーポンによる割引は客1人あたり商品いくつまで適用できますか。

_____

TOEIC Practice

Listening   Part 1, 3

Tips! Part 1 では聞こえてきた英文の内容が写真から客観的に判断できることなのかを意識してください。Part 3 は図表が含まれることがあります。会話のそれぞれの部分が図表のどこに対応しているのかを聴きながら同時に確認していきましょう。

Part 1 ⟳CheckLink 🎧DL 52 ◎CD2-07

Look at the picture and select the statement that best describes what you see in the picture.

1.

2.

(A) (B) (C) (D)   (A) (B) (C) (D)

Part 3 ⟳CheckLink 🎧DL 53 ◎CD2-08

Listen to the conversation while looking at the graphic and select the best response to each question.

Schedule, December 5		
Orchid Room, Window Table		
Dinner Seating Times	Name (number of people)	Phone Number
5:30	A. Grogan (3)	555-2958
7:00	K. Reyes (2)	555-1029
8:30		
10:00	J. Tabata (2)	555-8832
11:30 (drinks/snacks only)	K. Hayes (3)	555-9401

1. What does the woman ask the man to do?

   (A) Cancel her reservations altogether

   (B) Change her seating time

   (C) Move her away from the window

   (D) Reschedule her for another date

2. What does the woman offer to do?

   (A) Call back at another time

   (B) Come on another night

   (C) Order only drinks

   (D) Sit in a different place

3. Look at the graphic. What time did the woman originally book?

   (A) 5:30

   (B) 7:00

   (C) 10:00

   (D) 11:30

Tips!▶ Part 5 の動詞を選ぶ問題では、動作が完了したことなのか進行中のことなのか、あるいは（過去からの）継続なのかを文脈からよく見極めてください。動詞は能動態と受動態のどちらが適切かということも考える必要があります。Part 7 ではトリプルパッセージの場合、情報を統合して読み解く力が一段と要求されますが、日本語で文書を読むときと同じです。当事者になったつもりで丁寧に読み解きましょう。

Part 5   CheckLink   DL 54   CD2-09

Select the best answer to complete the sentence.

1. The team ------- a new menu for summer now.

(A) is discussing　　(B) discussing　　(C) had discussed　　(D) had been discussing

2. The guests were impressed by how beautifully the dishes ------- on the table.

(A) have been arranged　　　　　　(C) were arranging

(B) were arranged　　　　　　　　(D) have arranged

3. The restaurant chain ------- a plan to make vegetarian meals available yet.

(A) does not announce　　　　　　(C) has not been announced

(B) is announced　　　　　　　　(D) has not announced

4. A week ago, a dent ------- on the floor of the kitchen.

(A) is　　(B) is being　　(C) was found　　(D) has been found

5. This dish ------- the flagship item of our restaurant menu for five years.

(A) is being　　(B) has been　　(C) is　　(D) been

6. Please note that the dining room is now -------.

(A) renovate　　(B) renovating　　(C) being renovated　　(D) has renovated

7. Water ------- from the fountain, and people are enjoying lunch around it.

(A) spray　　(B) is being sprayed　　(C) spraying　　(D) had sprayed

8. We ------- the dinner show in a couple of minutes.

(A) will be starting　　(B) would have started　　(C) have started　　(D) started

9. Some employees were told to do the dishes while others ------- the new dish.

(A) taste　　(B) have tasted　　(C) were tasting　　(D) would taste

10. More and more hotels ------- guests with a sophisticated culinary experience.

(A) are trying to attract　　　　　　(C) will be attracted

(B) are being attracted　　　　　　(D) attracting

Part 7

CheckLink   DL 55   CD2-10

Questions 1-5 refer to the following advertisement, invoice, and e-mail.

 SANTOS TACOS CATERING

Santos Tacos wants to make your next event special by offering a unique and delicious Mexican food experience. We're available for parties of all sizes and are offering two different options for our customers:

Come to Us:

We provide platters of our famous tacos, as well as beans, rice, and a variety of salsas. You pick them up and take them to your event. We offer both hot and cold preparations. The price is determined per person, with three tacos per person being our usual estimate. Plates and flatware are not included but are available for an additional fee. Forty-eight-hour notice is required.

We Come to You:

We bring our taco cart to your event and cook the tacos there. Our clients consistently love how much fun their guests have watching tacos being made in front of them. Beans, rice, and salsas are included as well. As with our first option above, price is determined per person, and three tacos per person is our basic estimate. As a rule, the event must have a minimum of 40 people, but the number can be changed upon request. Plates and flatware are included. Must reserve two weeks in advance.

INVOICE

Santos Tacos Catering

1438 Elm Ave.
Rochester, MN
550-9030

Invoice Number: C00421
Invoice Date: August 2
Due Date: August 16

Bill To:
Harlan Mobley (Minnesota Central University)
253 Redwood St.
Rochester, MN
550-9023

Plan: We Come to You

Number of Guests:	35
Price Per Guest:	$30
Drink Surcharge:	$0
Dessert Surcharge:	$300
Amount Due:	$1,350

To:	santostacos@mail.net
From:	mobley@mcu.edu
Date:	August 3
Subject:	Catering Invoice Mistake

Hello,

First, I wanted to say I very much enjoyed the catering for the university we hired you for. Your ad was right about everyone enjoying the live cooking experience. Several people commented on it the next day at work. The food itself was excellent. We would certainly like to continue to patronize you in the future.

However, I do have a question about the invoice. We did not order any desserts with the service, but I see there is a surcharge for it listed. I assume this was made in error and would appreciate it if you would look into the matter.

Thank you,

Harlan Mobley, Minnesota Central University

1. What is required to reserve a "Come to Us" plan from the taco shop?

   (A) A certain size party

   (B) Two days' notice

   (C) A credit card

   (D) An e-mail address

2. In the advertisement, the word "preparations" in paragraph 2 line 3, is closest in meaning to

   (A) proceedings

   (B) states

   (C) arrangements

   (D) dishes

3. What point of the advertisement did Mr. Mobley agree with?

   (A) The price of food was very reasonable.

   (B) The catering is good for parties of any size.

   (C) Watching the cooking was entertaining.

   (D) The included desserts were unique.

4. What change did the restaurant make for Mr. Mobley?

   (A) They offered cold food service for an in-person event.

   (B) They did not charge him for the drinks he ordered.

   (C) They catered his event even though there were fewer people than required.

   (D) They accepted his reservation even though it was late.

5. How much less does Mr. Mobley expect to pay?

   (A) $30

   (B) $35

   (C) $300

   (D) $1,350

Complaint & Inquiry

受動態

Goal

・顧客から寄せられるクレームや問い合わせのパターンや英文の流れを理解する
・受動態のさまざまな形に対応できるようになる

 ## Warm-Up Questions 🎧 DL 56   ◎ CD2-11

日本語訳を参考に、空所に入る語を (A) ～ (D) から選びましょう。

1. あなたの注文品は発送されました。

   Your order -------.

   (A) will ship　　(B) will be shipped　　(C) has been shipped　　(D) ships

2. お問い合わせやクレームはさまざまな手段で行うことができます。

   Inquiries and complaints ------- through different channels.

   (A) is made　　(B) made　　(C) can be made　　(D) make

Words & Expressions 🎧 DL 57   ◎ CD2-12

音声を聞いて、日本語訳に合う語を（　　）内に書き入れましょう。

1. 特別な割引クーポン　　　　　　a special (**d** _ _ _ _ _ _ _) coupon
2. お詫びの印として　　　　　　　as a token of our (**a** _ _ _ _ _ _)
3. 渋滞した道路　　　　　　　　　a (**c** _ _ _ _ _ _ _ _) road
4. 返金してもらう　　　　　　　　get (**r** _ _ _ _ _ _ _ _ _)
5. 発表する　　　　　　　　　　　make an (**a** _ _ _ _ _ _ _ _ _ _ _)
6. 製品の正確な状態　　　　　　　the (**e** _ _ _ _) condition of the product
7. ヒビのある商品　　　　　　　　an item that is (**c** _ _ _ _ _ _)
8. 交換品を依頼する　　　　　　　ask for a (**r** _ _ _ _ _ _ _ _ _)
9. 問題を解決する　　　　　　　　(**r** _ _ _ _ _ _) an issue
10. 引っ越しの手続き　　　　　　　moving (**p** _ _ _ _ _ _ _ _)
11. その会社にEメールで連絡する　contact the company (**v** _ _) e-mail
12. 上司にEメールを転送する　　　(**f** _ _ _ _ _ _) an e-mail to the boss
13. 商品の見た目　　　　　　　　　the (**a** _ _ _ _ _ _ _ _ _) of the product
14. 欠陥のレベル　　　　　　　　　the level of (**d** _ _ _ _ _)
15. へこみが原因で　　　　　　　　because of the (**d** _ _ _)

Grammar Focus　　受動態

受動態は TOEIC L&R 頻出の文法項目です。時制や一緒に用いられる助動詞などに注意しましょう。熟語として定着した受動態表現も出題されます。

◎ 受動態の基本的な形を確認しておきましょう。

時制・助動詞	受動態の形
現在	is/am/are ＋過去分詞
現在進行	is/am/are ＋ being ＋過去分詞
過去	was/were ＋過去分詞
過去進行	was/were ＋ being ＋過去分詞
現在完了	have/has ＋ been ＋過去分詞
過去完了	had been ＋過去分詞
助動詞	助動詞＋ be ＋過去分詞

・「誰がするか」を明示したい場合は後ろに by ＋名詞を続けます。
　　例：You will be contacted by the personnel manager.
　　　　「人事部長から連絡があります」
・句動詞などの慣用表現も Part 1 や Part 5 の受動態の問題で頻出です。
　　例：Old furniture must be disposed of properly. ※前置詞を忘れないよう注意
　　　　「古い家具は適切に処分されなければなりません」

 Practice　　　　　　　　　　　　　　　 DL 58　　 CD2-13

空所に入る語句を語群から選び、文を完成させましょう。選択肢は一度しか使えません。

1. A bicycle ------- against the wall of the building.
2. Some people haven't ------- about this project.
3. A special discount coupon will ------- to you as a token of our apology.
4. No announcement has ------- about the release date.
5. The reception room ------- to capacity.
6. The roads ------- because of the event.
7. The issue is ------- now.
8. Multiple cardboard boxes ------- on top of each other.
9. This package may have ------- during shipping.
10. Kitchen utensils ------- on the table, but they were a little dirty.

A. is propped up	**B.** was filled	**C.** are stacked	**D.** were congested
E. being discussed	**F.** been informed	**G.** were arranged	
H. been dropped	**I.** be sent	**J.** been made	

 ## Short Listening

次の会話を聞いて、1 〜 4 の（　　）に語を書き入れましょう。そのあと、5 と 6 の質問に日本語で答えましょう。

M: Hello, this is Customer Service.

W: Hello. I'm calling because the fan I bought yesterday is (¹·　　　　　　). Can you please (²·　　　　　　) it for a new one?

M: Thank you for (³·　　　　　　) us. First of all, I would like to know the exact (⁴·　　　　　　) of the fan, so could you please answer a few questions for me?

---

5. 女性はなぜ電話をかけていますか。

6. 男性は女性に何を求めていますか。

 ## Short Reading

次のテキスト・メッセージのやりとりを読んで、1 〜 3 の質問に日本語で答えましょう。

> **Operator (9:46 A.M.):** Hello, Mr. Martinez. How may I help you today?

> **Adam Martinez (9:50 A.M.):** I ordered this vacuum cleaner on May 7, but as soon as I opened the package, I found that the hose was cracked.
> Not only that, the cleaner was delivered 12 days later than the expected arrival date. If it had been just a crack, I would have asked for a replacement. But since the delivery was late and the product is broken, I don't even want to ask for a replacement. Can I ship the item back to you and get reimbursed?

1. マルティネスさんの掃除機にはどのような問題がありますか。

2. 商品は予定よりもどのくらい遅れて到着しましたか。

3. マルティネスさんは購入した掃除機について、何を望んでいますか。

TOEIC Practice

Listening

Tips! Part 1 ではこれまでの Unit と同様、客観的に正しいと言えることは何かをよく意識し、推測で判断されるような内容は選ばないよう注意してください。Part 4 はオフィスに関するお知らせを聴き取ります。図表を参照しながら細かい情報を把握する練習をしましょう。

Part 1

 CheckLink   DL 61   CD2-16

Look at the picture and select the statement that best describes what you see in the picture.

1.

(A)   (B)   (C)   (D)

2.

(A)   (B)   (C)   (D)

Part 4

 CheckLink   DL 62   CD2-17

Listen to the talk while looking at the graphic and select the best response to each question.

Department	Location (after November 8)
Executive Offices / Operations	9F
Personnel	8F
Accounting	7F
Sales / Research & Development	6F

1. What is the main point of the announcement?
   (A) To suggest locations at which to meet with clients
   (B) To explain the importance of getting receipts for expenses
   (C) To tell employees about moving procedures
   (D) To describe new equipment

2. What does Mr. Reiner think is a good way to take advantage of this situation?
   (A) Staying home and work on expense reports
   (B) Having fun with relatives or pals
   (C) Going to a special seminar at a café
   (D) Inviting new clients to the office

3. Look at the graphic. What floor is Mr. Reiner's office currently on?
   (A) 6F   (B) 7F   (C) 8F   (D) 9F

Tips! Part 5 で動詞を選ぶ問題は、文全体を見て、主語との関係や時制に注意してください。また、試験では慣用表現もよく出題されますが、受動態の文法的な知識があると解答に役立つ場合があります。Part 6 はクレームの英文です。書き手がどのような問題を抱えているのか、問題の詳細や時系列はどうなっているか、どのような解決策を望んでいるかなどを読み解き、文脈に照らして適切な語句や文を挿入しましょう。

Part 5

CheckLink DL 63 CD2-18

Select the best answer to complete the sentence.

1. The issues the manager was worried about ------- via e-mail yesterday.

   (A) were resolved

   (B) are resolved

   (C) may be resolved

   (D) has been resolved

2. Inquiries about the new product ------- an hour ago.

   (A) has been made   (B) will be made   (C) were made   (D) had been made

3. Mr. Jones called customer service, but he ------- to wait for one hour.

   (A) told   (B) was told   (C) is told   (D) will be told

4. You ------- via e-mail soon after your inquiry about the damaged product has been received.

   (A) will contact   (B) contact   (C) will be contacted   (D) have been contacted

5. The company ------- for being slow to respond to the complaints of customers.

   (A) was being criticized   (B) criticized   (C) is criticizing   (D) can criticize

6. The customer was told that the suite ------- as per her request.

   (A) would be reserved

   (B) reserved

   (C) will have been reserved

   (D) is being reserved

7. You ------- by a sales representative when you get to headquarters.

   (A) were attended

   (B) will attend

   (C) attended

   (D) will be attended to

8. The new product is ------- at an incredible pace now.

   (A) to sell   (B) selling   (C) sells   (D) sell

9. It seems that your inquiry ------- to the department in charge yet.

   (A) will be forwarded

   (B) will forward

   (C) had not forwarded

   (D) has not been forwarded

10. The client was ------- for a long time even though she had made a reservation.

   (A) been waited   (B) made to wait   (C) had waited   (D) wait

Part 6

Questions 1- 4 refer to the following e-mail.

To: help@toraelectronics.com

From: felicia.dano@email.com

Date: March 20

Subject: Re: Recently Purchased Rice Cooker

Hello,

I'm writing to let you know about a few issues I've had with my new rice cooker.

When I first opened the box, I found that the side -------. It didn't seem to affect
1.
the performance of the appliance and concerned only its appearance, so I didn't

contact you immediately.

The main problem came later when I was ------- to use the timer function. It
2.
worked well the first time, but the second time it started cooking at the wrong

time. -------. I think a battery issue is causing this, and I can't change it -------. I've
3. **4.**
always enjoyed your products and would hate to stop using them after one bad

experience. With this level of defect, I think I will need a replacement rice cooker.

Felicia Dano

---

1. (A) will dent
   (B) is denting
   (C) was dented
   (D) will have been dented

2. (A) trying
   (B) tried
   (C) tries
   (D) try

3. (A) I had trouble understanding the
          cooking instructions.
   (B) I discovered that when unplugged
          the clock reset.
   (C) I had this same problem with one
          of your appliances before.
   (D) I haven't used the cooker with
          guests because of the dent.

4. (A) around here
   (B) so to say
   (C) by myself
   (D) on the whole

Review Test 1

Listening

Part 1

CheckLink　DL 65　CD2-20

Look at the picture and select the statement that best describes what you see in the picture.

1.

(A)　(B)　(C)　(D)

2.

(A)　(B)　(C)　(D)

Part 2

CheckLink　DL 66　CD2-21

Listen to the question or statement and the three responses. Then select the best response to each question or statement.

3. (A)　　(B)　　(C)
4. (A)　　(B)　　(C)
5. (A)　　(B)　　(C)
6. (A)　　(B)　　(C)
7. (A)　　(B)　　(C)
8. (A)　　(B)　　(C)

Part 3

C CheckLink   🎧 DL 67   ◎ CD2-22

Listen to the conversations and select the best response to each question.

9. What is the conversation mainly about?
   - (A) Visiting Miami
   - (B) Canceling a flight
   - (C) Asking for a discount
   - (D) Getting a credit card

10. Why does the woman have to pay a fee?
    - (A) Because Warwick Airways always charges this
    - (B) Because she had received a discount
    - (C) Because the departure date is quite soon
    - (D) Because she is not a premium member

11. How will the airline return the funds?
    - (A) They will transfer the money to her bank account.
    - (B) They will put money back on her credit card.
    - (C) They will mail a refund check to her home.
    - (D) They will send her special flight coupons.

Conference Room Schedule This Week

ROOM	CAPACITY	TUESDAY		WEDNESDAY	
		10–12 A.M.	2–5 P.M.	10–12 A.M.	2–5 P.M.
403	15	International		R&D	
404	20	R&D	Marketing	General Affairs	Personnel
405	18		Accounting		Accounting
406	12	General Affairs	Personnel		

12. Why is the man calling?
(A) To ask for some beverages
(B) To mention some special guests
(C) To move to a smaller room
(D) To request a schedule change

13. What does the woman suggest the man do?
(A) Use a room in the morning
(B) Move to a different room
(C) Fill in a form
(D) Call his colleague

14. Look at the graphic. Which department had scheduled the conference room for the time the man agrees to?
(A) General Affairs
(B) International
(C) Marketing
(D) R&D

Part 4

 CheckLink   DL 69   CD2-24

Listen to the talks and select the best response to each question.

15. What kind of company does the speaker work for?
   (A) A telephone company
   (B) A media provider
   (C) An insurance company
   (D) A home security company

16. Why is the speaker leaving a message?
   (A) He is returning Ms. Bronstein's call.
   (B) He wants to arrange an appointment.
   (C) Ms. Bronstein is eligible for a discount.
   (D) Nobody was home when he visited.

17. How will Ms. Bronstein likely respond to the message?
   (A) She will return Mr. Fletcher's call right away.
   (B) She will call to speak with Mr. Fletcher's superior.
   (C) She will go online to answer a company survey.
   (D) She will only respond if she has more issues.

Crawford Department Store

Annual Super Sale

25% off all sleepwear	Reg. $18–98	Sale $13.50–73.50
30% off fashion jewelry	Reg. $14–55	Sale $9.80–38.50
50% off women's sweaters	Reg. $40–68	Sale $20–34

Capture the code or go to crawfordept.com/sale for an extra discount.

18. What does the speaker imply is different about this sale?

(A) It is possible to do the shopping online.

(B) It is the last year they will hold this sale.

(C) There is a new increase in the discounts.

(D) There is much more inventory than usual.

19. Look at the graphic. What is the maximum amount that someone can save on a women's sweater?

(A) 25%

(B) 35%

(C) 50%

(D) 60%

20. What does the speaker say about returning merchandise?

(A) It is not possible to return an item purchased at a discount.

(B) Returns may be possible for certain special reasons.

(C) Shoppers may return purchases for a limited time.

(D) There is no set policy about bringing merchandise back.

Reading

Part 5

CheckLink DL 71 CD2-26

Select the best answer to complete the sentence.

21. We are grateful to Mr. Tanaka for ------- dedication.

(A) he   (B) him   (C) he's   (D) his

22. All employees are required to act -------.

(A) responsibility   (B) response   (C) responsibly   (D) responsible

23. Please note that the call center will not be available ------- the construction is taking place.

(A) in   (B) during   (C) between   (D) while

24. Everyone thought the meeting would be postponed ------- the end of the month.

(A) when   (B) on   (C) with   (D) until

25. It ------- announced yesterday that Ms. Smith would be promoted to section chief.

(A) is   (B) was   (C) has been   (D) had been

26. Servers ------- on the second floor of the headquarters building.

(A) are being replaced   (B) replacing   (C) are replacing   (D) replace

27. The shopping center ------- relocated to Winston Avenue next year.

(A) has been   (B) could have been   (C) will be   (D) should have been

28. The manager has been working on the materials for his presentation ------- the past five hours.

(A) on   (B) until   (C) during   (D) for

Attention: Retirement Farewell Party This Friday

I'd like to invite everyone to a retirement farewell party this Friday at 6 P.M. on Ryuichi Tadano's last day at the company. Ryuichi has worked in our finance department for over 30 years, and we want to give ------- a good send-off. The
29.
party will take place in nearby Dove Park, and I've attached a map for those who haven't been there.

Food and drinks have already -------, so there is no need to bring anything.
30.
However, Ryuichi is a great dog lover, ------- if you would like to bring your dog,
31.
please feel free to do so. -------. We hope to see you all there to say farewell to
32.
one of our longest-serving employees!

---

29. (A) their
   (B) him
   (C) it
   (D) he

30. (A) was purchased
   (B) been purchased
   (C) will purchase
   (D) being purchased

31. (A) so
   (B) but
   (C) nor
   (D) because

32. (A) The park allows pets as long as they are on a leash.
   (B) The marketing team will miss Tadano's great work.
   (C) Just one snack per person should be enough for the meal.
   (D) After the party you can head to the office to start the day.

Part 7

Questions 33-35 refer to the following notice.

MEET THE AUTHOR
Sophia de Campos

This Friday, come to see author Sophia de Campos in a seminar where she will have a conversation with Biology professor Dr. Thomas Galatas about her fourth book, "Everything You Didn't Know About Animals." De Campos has achieved recognition for her books that teach science in an approachable and easy-to-understand way. Her last book, "You Are What You Eat," received the National Prize for Popular Science Books and was a national bestseller. De Campos will be reading excerpts from her latest book and hosting a Q&A session afterwards. If you would like your question answered, please submit it on a card before the seminar begins. Seating will be limited, so sign up on the university Web site or call 555-840-0284.

33. What does the article mention about de Campos' books?
    (A) They are usually about new research.
    (B) They are popular with teachers.
    (C) They are meant for older readers.
    (D) They are for non-scientists to read.

34. What is mentioned about de Campos' previous book?
    (A) It was about animals.
    (B) It was her first book.
    (C) It wasn't very long.
    (D) It won an award.

35. Which will NOT be a portion of the seminar?
    (A) A science demonstration
    (B) Reading book passages
    (C) Answering questions
    (D) A conversation with an expert

Questions 36-40 refer to the following job advertisement and e-mail.

Help Wanted — Car Mechanic

Twinning Motors needs a new car mechanic to join its team of dedicated experts to offer superior service to our customers. We are a thriving company with many clients and a steady stream of work. Applicants will be expected to quickly integrate with our workforce with minimal training. For that reason we are only interested in experienced mechanics.

We service all kinds of cars at Twinnings, so we are not looking for certification for any particular manufacturer. However, we appreciate seeing any training you have.

Required skills:
-Brakes, wheels, and tires
-Diagnostics
-Safety inspections
-Engine work
-Oil and fluid changes

Five years of experience is preferred, and access to your own tools is a must.

Contact Brenda Ross at ross@twinningmotors.net to apply.

To:	Brenda Ross <ross@twinningmotors.net>
From:	Shelly Cooper <shelly89@starmail.com>
Date:	April 3
Subject:	Mechanic Job Opening

Dear Ms. Ross,

Hello, my name is Shelly Cooper, and I would like to apply for the mechanic position you just posted. I have been working as a mechanic for six years at a dealership in town and was looking to switch positions. I have been in charge of diagnostics and safety inspections, but working on the same manufacturer's cars all the time is becoming a little tedious, and I wanted to use more of my creativity when working. Looking at your business I am confident my skills would be a good fit for you, even though I don't yet have a full collection of tools.

Since I have worked at a Catamount dealership, I have certification for working on their cars. I also have a good deal of experience with other manufacturers as well by working on them outside of work. I very often work on the cars of my friends, which has allowed me to hone my skills on a wide variety of cars for several years. It has exposed me to automobiles of all types and from all countries and has made me a more versatile mechanic.

Thank you for your consideration,

Shelly Cooper

36. What does the job listing say about training for the job?

    (A) It will last between two to three weeks.

    (B) Only those without certification need it.

    (C) New hires will not be paid during it.

    (D) There will not be a great amount of it.

37. What is NOT listed as a desired attribute for the job?

    (A) Focused experience with a single manufacturer

    (B) Working on engines

    (C) Having your own tools to bring to work

    (D) Several years of prior experience

38. Why does Ms. Cooper want to change where she works?

    (A) She finds her place of work boring.

    (B) She wants a slower pace of work.

    (C) She is not being paid enough.

    (D) She is making more working alone.

39. How did Ms. Cooper learn to work on all types of cars?

    (A) By taking various mechanic classes

    (B) By getting many different certifications

    (C) By working for several dealerships

    (D) By repairing the cars of people she knows

40. What requirements does Ms. Cooper not meet?

    (A) Five years of experience

    (B) Access to her own tools

    (C) Safety inspections

    (D) Diagnostics

Unit 8 Personnel

to 不定詞

Goal

・TOEIC L&R に頻出の人事に関する必須語彙・表現を学習し、関連する英文を処理する力を付ける
・to 不定詞の頻出問題をすばやく解けるように、さまざまな用法に触れ、知識を再確認する

Warm-Up Questions

日本語訳を参考に、空所に入る語を（A）～（D）から選びましょう。

1. 応募者が記入すべきフォームが 2 つあります。

   There are two forms ------- applicants to fill in.

   (A) with　　(B) for　　(C) so　　(D) as

2. 私たちはいつでも喜んで履歴書の改善をお手伝いします。

   We are glad ------- help you polish your résumé.

   (A) to　　(B) for　　(C) in　　(D) of

Words & Expressions

音声を聞いて、日本語訳に合う語を（　　）内に書き入れましょう。

1. 面接の段階に進む　　　　　　　（ **p** _ _ _ _ _ _ ）to the interview stage
2. そのポジションに応募する　　　（ **a** _ _ _ _ ）for the position
3. 素晴らしい加入人材　　　　　　a great（ **a** _ _ _ _ _ _ _ ）
4. 新入社員向けの研修　　　　　　a workshop for new（ **e** _ _ _ _ _ _ _ _ ）
5. 求人広告　　　　　　　　　　　a job（ **a** _ ）
6. ディレクターに昇進する　　　　be（ **p** _ _ _ _ _ _ _ ）to director
7. 経験を積んだ営業担当　　　　　an（ **e** _ _ _ _ _ _ _ _ _ _ ）salesperson
8. スタッフを管理する　　　　　　（ **m** _ _ _ _ _ ）the staff
9. 会計の求人　　　　　　　　　　a job opening in（ **a** _ _ _ _ _ _ _ _ _ ）
10. 最高執行責任者　　　　　　　　（ **C** _ _ _ _ ）Operating Officer
11. 正式な確認　　　　　　　　　　the official（ **c** _ _ _ _ _ _ _ _ _ _ _ ）
12. 彼女の在職期間の間に　　　　　during her（ **t** _ _ _ _ _ ）
13. 彼の現在の立場　　　　　　　　his（ **c** _ _ _ _ _ ）position
14. 事業を引き継ぐ　　　　　　　　（ **t** _ _ _ ）over operations
15. 率先して取り組む人　　　　　　a person of（ **i** _ _ _ _ _ _ _ _ _ ）

Grammar Focus   to 不定詞

to 不定詞にはさまざまな用法がありますが、TOEIC L&R で特に重要なのは (1) 名詞としての用法と、(2) 情報を補足する用法です。

(1) 名詞としての用法

「〜すること」という意味をもち、主語や目的語になります。

・主語の場合

例： To show your enthusiasm is the key to success.
　　「熱意を示すことが成功への鍵です」

・目的語の場合

目的語に to 不定詞をとる動詞があります。代表例をいくつか挙げます。

want, hope, refuse, decide, agree, expect, plan, promise, attempt, manage, wish

(2) 情報を補足する用法

文脈によって、理由や目的、用途などの意味をもちます。

例： We are happy to inform you that you will be promoted.〈理由〉
　　「あなたが昇進することを喜んでお伝えします」

　　Please fill in the form to apply for this position.〈目的〉
　　「このポジションに応募するためにフォームに記入してください」

　　Our company cafeteria is a good place to take a break.〈用途〉
　　「当社の社員食堂は一休みするのにいい場所です」

◈ Practice

🎧 DL 77　　 CD2-32

空所に入る語を語群から選び、文を完成させましょう。選択肢は一度しか使えません。

1. Please don't ------- to contact the personnel department.
2. We are ------- to inform you that you will be proceeding to the interview stage.
3. We are happy to ------- with you.
4. His CV leaves nothing to be -------.
5. We have five people to -------.
6. She is the youngest person ------- to become a general manager in our company.
7. Successful applicants are ------- to speak more than two languages fluently.
8. I understand ------- it means to be part of this company.
9. Thank you for giving me this great ------- to speak with you.
10. He will be a great addition ------- this project to succeed.

A. work	**B.** interview	**C.** hesitate	**D.** ever	**E.** for
F. what	**G.** happy	**H.** opportunity	**I.** desired	**J.** expected

72

Short Listening

DL 78　CD2-33

次の話を聞いて、1～4の（　　）に語を書き入れましょう。そのあと、5と6の質問に
日本語で答えましょう。

M: Thank you all for (¹.　　　　　　) here. I have planned this workshop for all

new (².　　　　　　　　). Aren't you anxious about what you will be

doing in this department? In this workshop, you will learn about basic

operations, such as how to (³.　　　　　　　) to customer inquiries. You will

learn from a (⁴.　　　　　) of case studies and will get yourself ready to

start your work here.

---

5. この話の聞き手は誰ですか。

_____

6. このワークショップで学ぶことの具体例は何ですか。

_____

Short Reading

DL 79　CD2-34

次のEメールを読んで、1～3の質問に日本語で答えましょう。

To whom it may concern,

Hello, my name is Thomas Frazer. I saw the job ad on your Web site, and I
am writing to find out more about the management position in the accounting
department. I have 10 years of experience in the field, and I believe I would be a
great addition to your company.

Looking forward to hearing from you.

Sincerely,

Thomas Frazer

---

1. どの部署の求人が公募されていますか。

_____

2. フレーザーさんはどの分野で、どのくらいの期間の経験がありますか。

_____

3. フレーザーさんは何を確信していますか。

_____

Listening

Tips! Part 2 では、相手の発言に対して意見や感想を述べる表現が出題されることがあります。発言をよく聞いて、やりとりとして成立するものはどれかを意識しましょう。Part 4 は発言の文字通りの意味だけでなく、その発言から暗示されていることや推測できることまで踏み込んで理解することが求められます。

Part 2

CheckLink DL 80 CD2-35

Listen to the question or statement and the three responses. Then select the best response to each question or statement.

1. (A)   (B)   (C)
2. (A)   (B)   (C)
3. (A)   (B)   (C)

Part 4

CheckLink DL 81 CD2-36

Listen to the talk and select the best response to each question.

1. Where does this announcement probably take place?
   (A) At a welcoming party for new employees
   (B) At a meeting of pharmaceutical company CEOs
   (C) Before a group of recently promoted employees
   (D) During a training workshop seminar for sales staff

2. Why does the woman say, "I'm sure many people feel the same"?
   (A) To reassure the employees
   (B) To make everyone competitive
   (C) To solve all of the problems
   (D) To manage an event

3. What will be the main purpose of the workshop?
   (A) To celebrate the promotions of new managers
   (B) To help new managers prepare to open offices
   (C) To develop new products
   (D) To allow new employees to get to know each other

Reading

Tips! ▶ Part 5 では、to 不定詞のどの用法や定型表現が問われているのか、出題の意図を選択肢から検討し、文脈と文法の両面から手際良く判断してください。Part 7 では、TOEIC L&R で頻出の人事に関わる英文を読みます。今回は指示語にも十分に注意を払ってください。

Part 5

CheckLink **DL 82** **CD2-37**

Select the best answer to complete the sentence.

1. Our boss was ------- engaged with work to notice other employees coming in.
(A) so   (B) enough   (C) too   (D) very

2. The employee was not experienced ------- to handle the situation.
(A) enough   (B) so   (C) too   (D) order

3. It was kind ------- the manager to give everyone at the company a thank-you gift.
(A) in   (B) for   (C) with   (D) of

4. It has never been easy ------- anyone to manage a large number of tasks at the same time.
(A) of   (B) to   (C) for   (D) in

5. Successful applicants are ------- to have a master's degree in finance.
(A) need   (B) required   (C) suppose   (D) enough

6. I had a clear idea of ------- after I had been chosen as manager.
(A) what to do   (B) how to do   (C) when to do   (D) where to do

7. Employees should have the ability to figure out ------- handle the pressure.
(A) what to   (B) how to   (C) as to   (D) enough to

8. The sales department has announced a plan ------- hire several new staff members.
(A) to   (B) with   (C) of   (D) on

9. In order ------- well, we need to have a sales expert on staff.
(A) for our product to sell   (C) for our product selling
(B) our product to sell   (D) for our product sale

10. Mr. Davis was very fortunate ------- as a sales representative for the company.
(A) to choose   (C) to have been chosen
(B) to be choosing   (D) for him to choose

Part 7

Questions **1-3** refer to the following article.

Corneja Selects Internal Employee for COO

BOSTON (23 May)—Local company Corneja Hardware announced the promotion of Maria Cisneros as their Chief Operating Officer.

The announcement, which was regarded as an open secret for some time before the official confirmation, came after the departure of previous COO Katherine Herrera. — [1] —. In the announcement Corneja stated its preference for promoting internally, and Ms. Cisneros is a long-time employee of the company. She started her tenure at the company as a low-level employee in the shipping department and worked her way up to her current position. — [2] —.

Ms. Cisneros will be taking over operations for the third-highest selling manufacturer of hand tools in the country. — [3] —. The corporation was founded in 1949 by Miguel Toro, who wanted to make a company that offered professional-level tools to people who used them as a hobby instead of a job. — [4] —.

1. What is implied about the new announcement?
   (A) Some people knew about it already.
   (B) It has been delayed for some time.
   (C) Most people wouldn't expect it.
   (D) The company had to make it soon.

2. What does the article say about Ms. Cisneros' career?
   (A) She joined the family business.
   (B) She started in a small position.
   (C) She worked at another company.
   (D) She had had this position before.

3. In which of the positions marked [1], [2], [3], and [4] does the following sentence best belong?

   "The company also praised her skill and initiative at every level."
   (A) [1]
   (B) [2]
   (C) [3]
   (D) [4]

Unit 9 Travel

分詞

Goal

・頻出の分野である旅行・移動に関する語彙や表現を幅広くおさえ、このテーマの英文への対応力を強化する

・現在分詞・過去分詞の用法と違いをよく理解し、分詞が文中でどのような働きをしているか理解する

Warm-Up Questions 　 DL 84　 CD2-39

日本語訳を参考に、空所に入る語を (A) ～ (D) から選びましょう。

1. 高く評価されている写真家であるトニー・ブラウンさんはトラベル・マガジン誌に寄稿しています。

Tony Brown, a highly ------- photographer, contributes articles to *Travel Magazine*.

(A) acclaim　　(B) acclaimed　　(C) acclaims　　(D) acclaiming

2. そのホテルには海を見わたすスイートルームが3つあります。

The hotel has three suites ------- a view of the ocean.

(A) command　　(B) commanded　　(C) commanding　　(D) commands

Words & Expressions 　 DL 85　 CD2-40

音声を聞いて、日本語訳に合う語を（　　）内に書き入れましょう。

1. 壮大な景色　　　　　　　　　a magnificent (**v** _ _ _)

2. 夕食を出す　　　　　　　　　(**s** _ _ _ _) dinner

3. 素晴らしい食事　　　　　　　(**a** _ _ _ _ _ _) meals

4. 迂回する　　　　　　　　　　make a (**d** _ _ _ _ _)

5. サンフランシスコをお勧めする　(**r** _ _ _ _ _ _ _ _) San Francisco

6. 文化の多様性　　　　　　　　the cultural (**d** _ _ _ _ _ _ _ _)

7. 息をのむような風景　　　　　(**b** _ _ _ _ _ _ _ _ _ _) scenery

8. 贅沢な時間　　　　　　　　　(**l** _ _ _ _ _ _ _) time

9. 私が思っていたより高値な　　more expensive than I (**e** _ _ _ _ _ _ _)

10. 洗練された都市での経験　　　a (**s** _ _ _ _ _ _ _ _ _ _ _) city experience

11. 田舎でのツアー　　　　　　　a tour in the (**c** _ _ _ _ _ _ _ _ _ _)

12. 国立博物館　　　　　　　　　a (**n** _ _ _ _ _ _ _) museum

13. 自然を探索する　　　　　　　(**e** _ _ _ _ _ _) nature

14. 海を見下ろす　　　　　　　　(**o** _ _ _ _ _ _ _) the ocean

15. 必見の行き先　　　　　　　　a (**m** _ _ _ - _ _ _) destination

Grammar Focus   分詞の頻出用法

分詞に関して特におさえておくべきポイントは (1) 名詞を修飾する用法と (2) 分詞構文の 2 つです。現在分詞と過去分詞それぞれについて確認しましょう。

◎ 現在分詞

(1) 名詞を修飾

The building **standing** next to the station is a newly opened shopping mall.

(2) 分詞構文

Seeing the beautiful river, I felt alive.

◎ 過去分詞

(1) 名詞を修飾

The article **written** about the new amusement park was amazing.

(2) 分詞構文

Asked to move to a suite, the guest was quite pleased.

［発展］分詞構文で主節よりも前の内容を表す場合は、〈Having ＋過去分詞〉を用います。

Having traveled around the world, she writes a lot of great travel articles.

Practice

  DL 86   CD2-41

空所に入る語を語群から選び、文を完成させましょう。選択肢は一度しか使えません。

1. The dinner ------- at the restaurant on the top floor of the hotel was amazing.

2. The pottery works ------- in this museum were all created by local artists.

3. Highly ------- in this field, the magazine has a strong influence on travelers.

4. The view from the top of the mountain is magnificent, ------- a lot of visitors from many different countries.

5. Please visit our souvenir shop ------- on the second floor.

6. The hotel has been attracting foreign visitors with a completely ------- interior.

7. Yesterday there was heavy rain in the area, ------- us to make a detour.

8. Participants will enjoy the tour with our ------- tour guide.

9. When you arrive at the airport, you will see a man ------- an information board.

10. The person ------- at the ticket office is our new business advisor.

A. forcing	**B.** served	**C.** recognized	**D.** experienced	**E.** holding
F. waiting	**G.** displayed	**H.** redesigned	**I.** attracting	**J.** located

Short Listening
DL 87　CD2-42

次の会話を聞いて、1〜4の（　　）に語を書き入れましょう。そのあと、5と6の質問に日本語で答えましょう。

M: Have you already (1.　　　　　　　　) where you're going on your trip next month?

W: No, I haven't decided yet. There are so many places I want to go (2.　　　　　) it's hard to decide.

M: I can understand how you feel. Personally, I would recommend San Francisco.

W: The fact is I'd always (3.　　　　　　　) to visit the West Coast of the U.S., so I went to San Francisco last year (4.　　　　　　) to experience the cultural diversity that characterizes the city.

5. 女性はなぜ来月旅行に行く場所を決めていないのですか。

6. 女性はサンフランシスコで何を経験しようと思ったのですか。

Short Reading
DL 88　CD2-43

次のレビューを読んで、1〜3の質問に日本語で答えましょう。

★★★★★ Coby Brian / posted on Aug 2

Last week, I stayed at the Southport Hotel overlooking the ocean, and the experience there was great. The layout of the room was perfect. The room also offered a breathtaking view of the sea. I also need to mention my food experience. The food was all delicious, tailored to meet the needs of every guest. If you are looking for a relaxing, luxurious time with your family, this hotel is highly recommended. You won't regret staying here.

1. この文章はおそらくどのような人に向けて書かれたものですか。

2. このホテルの立地についてどのようなことが述べられていますか。

3. ブライアンさんは、このホテルの食べ物のどのような点を評価していますか。

Listening

Tips! Part 1 でものだけが写っている写真が出題されたときは、人を主語にした進行形は原則不正解であることはコツとして知っておきましょう。人が写っている場合でも、選択肢の英文がその人の動作を正確に表したものであるかを慎重に検討してください。Part 3 では旅行の場面設定のカジュアルな会話のやりとりにトライします。短く口語的な表現も多く、全てを聞き取るのは難しいかもしれませんが、何を話題にしていて、どのようなやりとりをしているのか、大まかな流れを意識して聴きましょう。

Part 1

CheckLink　DL 89　CD2-44

Look at the picture and select the statement that best describes what you see in the picture.

1.

(A)　(B)　(C)　(D)

2.

(A)　(B)　(C)　(D)

Part 3

CheckLink　DL 90　CD2-45

Listen to the conversation and select the best response to each question.

1. What are the speakers discussing?
   (A) Whether or not they will eat at Mario's
   (B) Whether to check with the woman's sister
   (C) The type of food Mario's has on their menu
   (D) If Mario's is open on national holidays

2. Where is this conversation probably taking place?
   (A) At a train station
   (B) At a national museum
   (C) In front of a restaurant
   (D) At a man's house

3. What does the man mean when he says, "She said it was more expensive than she'd expected"?
   (A) He is interested in going to the restaurant.
   (B) He has other recommendations.
   (C) He is reluctant to go there.
   (D) He has never tried Mario's before.

Reading

Tips! Part 5 では、分詞が文の中で意味・文法の観点からどのような役割を果たしているのかをよく見極めてください。まずは意味の点で考えて、そして選んだものが文法的に問題がないかをチェックするという手順がよいでしょう。Part 6 はより文脈が多く与えられた空所補充と考えましょう。文法だけでなく、文章全体の流れをよく意識してください。

Part 5

 CheckLink DL 91 CD2-46

Select the best answer to complete the sentence.

1. Costa Hotel always loves to see guests ------- themselves.
   (A) enjoys   (B) to enjoy   (C) enjoyed   (D) enjoying

2. ------- at the center of the city, our hotel is your best choice in Vancouver.
   (A) Located   (B) Location   (C) Locates   (D) Locating

3. We have a lot of tour options, ------- from a sophisticated city experience to a relaxing nature tour in the countryside.
   (A) ranging   (B) to range   (C) ranges   (D) ranged

4. We had a good time ------- nature.
   (A) explores   (B) exploration   (C) explore   (D) exploring

5. You should not make a long list of things to do when -------.
   (A) travel   (B) traveling   (C) traveled   (D) to travel

6. You will definitely enjoy our ------- tour.
   (A) guided   (B) guiding   (C) guide   (D) guides

7. ------- in Malta for two weeks, Mr. Olsen knows some good restaurants there.
   (A) Having stayed   (B) Stayed   (C) To have stayed   (D) To stay

8. First-time visitors often have a hard time ------- out the best nightlife attractions in Barcelona.
   (A) figuring   (B) figure   (C) figured   (D) figures

9. The children were happy to see a lot of animals ------- in the wild.
   (A) lives   (B) living   (C) lived   (D) to live

10. Once ------- a one-day tram pass, the students will be able to travel around the city.
    (A) giving   (B) is given   (C) have been given   (D) given

Part 6

Questions 1-4 refer to the following article.

RIVERWOOD (September 7) — Penny Harbor has quickly become a must-see destination for tourists across the country. People are always ------- new reasons
1.
to visit this charming seaside village. The nearby beaches have been popular with visitors for decades, but there's more than just ocean fun for visitors.

There are pear and apple orchards nearby, offering scenic views for picnics and hikes. Many of them offer ------- plans that let you pay a set price and have
2.
as much fruit as you like. Others offer tours of cider making facilities that offer tastings.

The city also features a museum ------- to the artist Teressa Sanborn and housed
3.
in her old residence. There are also plaques around the town pointing out the subjects of some of her most famous paintings.

-------.
4.

---

1. (A) finds
(B) find
(C) finding
(D) found

2. (A) step-by-step
(B) all-you-can-eat
(C) side-by-side
(D) one-on-one

3. (A) dedicated
(B) dedicate
(C) dedicates
(D) dedicating

4. (A) Teressa Sandborn spent most of her early career working in New York City.
(B) Visitors are required to pay a parking fee at this parking lot.
(C) Lovers of both nature and the arts will all find something to enjoy in Penny Harbor.
(D) There are both alcoholic and non-alcoholic ciders available for purchase.

Unit 10 Business

動名詞

Goal

・TOEIC L&R で最も多く出題されるビジネス全般の場面設定に関する幅広い語彙や表現を学習する
・動名詞の頻出用法に習熟し、特に慣用的な表現を得点源にする

Warm-Up Questions

 DL 93　　 CD3-02

日本語訳を参考に、空所に入る語を (A) ～ (D) から選びましょう。

1. 働きすぎることは健康によくありません。

   ------- too hard is not good for your health.

   (A) Work　　　(B) Works　　　(C) Working　　　(D) Be working

2. ウィーゲルさんはシアトルに出張したことをいまだにはっきりと覚えています。

   Mr. Weigel still vividly remembers ------- in Seattle on business.

   (A) to stay　　　(B) staying　　　(C) to have stayed　　　(D) stay

Words & Expressions

DL 94　　 CD3-03

音声を聞いて、日本語訳に合う語を（　　）内に書き入れましょう。

1. 誰にも負けない　　　　　　　　　　(s _ _ _ _ _) to none
2. お客様の満足　　　　　　　　　　　the (s _ _ _ _ _ _ _ _ _ _ _) of our customers
3. お客様のニーズに応える　　　　　　(r _ _ _ _ _ _) to customer needs
4. 社内研修　　　　　　　　　　　　　an (i _ - _ _ _ _ _) training session
5. 情報を整理する　　　　　　　　　　(o _ _ _ _ _ _ _) information
6. 上司に報告する　　　　　　　　　　report to my (s _ _ _ _ _ _ _ _ _)
7. 混乱が生じるのを避ける　　　　　　(a _ _ _ _) causing confusion
8. 会社を経営する　　　　　　　　　　(m _ _ _ _ _) a firm
9. 他社と合併する　　　　　　　　　　(m _ _ _ _) with another company
10. 書類を提出する　　　　　　　　　　(s _ _ _ _ _) a document
11. 懸命に働く従業員　　　　　　　　　a (h _ _ _ _ _ _ _ _ _ _) employee
12. 研修プログラムを受ける　　　　　　(u _ _ _ _ _ _) a training program
13. 経験に応じて変わる　　　　　　　　(v _ _ _) depending on experience
14. カスタマーサービスに従事する　　　be (i _ _ _ _ _ _ _) in customer service
15. そのポジションの候補者　　　　　　a (c _ _ _ _ _ _ _ _) for the position

Grammar Focus 動名詞の最頻出事項

動名詞は「〜すること」という意味を表し、主語・補語・目的語になります。ここでは、いくつかの用法や慣用表現について把握しましょう。

◎特定の動詞の目的語として：「〜すること」を表す方法として to 不定詞の名詞的用法がありますが、動詞によって、to 不定詞を目的語にとるのか、動名詞を目的語にとるのかが異なります。ここでは動名詞を目的語にとる代表的な動詞を挙げます。

admit, avoid, consider, miss, forgive, mind, imagine, finish, practice, enjoy, appreciate, suggest, discuss, complete, delay, resist, recommend, keep, postpone, deny, anticipate

◎動名詞の意味上の主語：意味上の主語を表すときは動名詞の前に名詞・代名詞の目的格か所有格をおきます。

例：Would you mind me[my] staying here?「ここにいてもよいですか」

◎過去を表す：「〜したこと」という意味を表すときは having ＋過去分詞を用います。

例：I apologize for having missed the deadline.「締め切りに遅れて申し訳ありません」

◎頻出の慣用表現の例：in -ing「〜する際に」、when it comes to -ing「〜することとなると」、insist on -ing「〜することを強く求める」

慣用表現については頻出のものを問題演習の中でおさえましょう。

 # Practice DL 95　 CD3-04

空所に入る語句を語群から選び、文を完成させましょう。選択肢は一度しか使えません。なお、文頭に来る語も小文字で与えられています。

1. He is second to none when it comes to ------- the efficiency of a project.
2. We ------- making improvements for the satisfaction of our customers.
3. She insisted on ------- participating in the exhibition.
4. We need to go over this document before ------- a meeting with the client.
5. I apologize for ------- to return your e-mail right away.
6. The customer mentioned ------- excited by the service.
7. Making sure you promptly answer e-mails is important ------- of your customers.
8. It was a great pleasure ------- with you.
9. Mr. Suzuki is good at ------- interior-related products.
10. ------- to respond to customer requests at any time is our top priority.

A. improving	**B.** having	**C.** being able	**D.** developing
E. me	**F.** take pride in	**G.** in maintaining the trust	
H. having been	**I.** talking	**J.** not being able	

Short Listening

次の話を聞いて、1〜4の（　　）に語を書き入れましょう。そのあと、5と6の質問に
日本語で答えましょう。

W: Thank you for (¹·　　　　　　　　） to the lecture today. Our speaker for today is
Professor Sandra Chen, who is well known for (²·　　　　　　　　）
productivity in business. She has recently published a book on
(³·　　　　　　　　） information in an efficient and relevant manner.
Today's talk will focus on (⁴·　　　　　　　　） tasks and improving
workflow, which will definitely benefit all of us.

---

5. チェン教授は何の研究をしていますか。

_____

6. 今回の講演のトピックは何ですか。

_____

Short Reading

次の案内を読んで、1〜3の質問に日本語で答えましょう。

Dear employees,

There will be an in-house training session on compliance on Monday, June 10,
in Conference Room 4. The focus of this session will be on handling confidential
information and securing sensitive data. If you are unable to attend due to work
schedule reasons, please be sure to report to your supervisor. The same training
session will be held again at a later date in the same month for the purpose of
providing an equal opportunity to participate, and you will be required to attend on
the make-up day.

Sincerely,

Sarah Lynd

---

1. この法令遵守についての研修では何を学びますか。

_____

2. 参加できない場合はまず何をすべきですか。

_____

3. 同じ研修はいつ行われますか。

_____

Listening

Tips! Part 2 では動名詞の入った慣用表現を聞いて理解できるか試してみましょう。慣用表現は覚えているか、知っているかが全てです。瞬発的に意味が分かるものが増えれば得点アップは間違いありません。Part 4 は図表問題に取り組みましょう。音声を聴きながら、図表を参照し情報を処理する力は、実生活でも非常に大切です。

Part 2

CheckLink DL 98 CD3-07

Listen to the question or statement and the three responses. Then select the best response to each question or statement.

1. (A)   (B)   (C)
2. (A)   (B)   (C)
3. (A)   (B)   (C)

Part 4

CheckLink DL 99 CD3-08

Listen to the talk while looking at the graphic and select the best response to each question.

 Supersonic Speakers

New! Pink Diamond Speaker
    — Perfect for home use
Blue Diamond Speaker
    — Waterproof and durable

Black Diamond Speaker
    — Great for outdoor listening
White Diamond Speaker
    — For classical music lovers

1. Where does the speaker most likely work?
   (A) At a recording studio
   (B) At a travel agency
   (C) At an audio equipment manufacturer
   (D) At a shipping company

2. What kind of technology do the Supersonic Speakers use?
   (A) Surround sound technology
   (B) Wireless technology
   (C) Unpatented technology
   (D) Anti-noise technology

3. Look at the graphic. If someone didn't want to spend a lot of money on speakers, which one would they most likely choose?
   (A) The Pink Diamond
   (B) The Black Diamond
   (C) The Blue Diamond
   (D) The White Diamond

Reading

Tips! Part 5 では、動名詞をとる動詞や動名詞を含む慣用表現などを「覚えているかどうか」が勝負です。また、動名詞の性質を問う問題も多く出題されます。Part 7 は TOEIC L&R 最頻出ともいえる求人関係の場面設定です。大まかな出題傾向を把握しましょう。

Part 5

ↄCheckLink   DL 100   CD3-09

Select the best answer to complete the sentence.

1. To avoid ------- confusion, make the instruction manual as detailed as possible.
   (A) causing   (B) to cause   (C) caused   (D) causes

2. Ms. Yamasaki needs to go back to the office because she remembered something that she forgot -------.
   (A) to do   (B) did   (C) do   (D) done

3. ------- a firm is hard work, especially one with a staff of thousands.
   (A) Manage   (B) Management   (C) Manages   (D) Managing

4. Mr. Hansen suggested ------- the launch of a new line of smartphones.
   (A) postpone   (B) postponing   (C) to postpone   (D) for postponing

5. The sales representative extended her sincere apology for ------- more quickly.
   (A) not having responded   (C) have not responded
   (B) not to respond   (D) response

6. Ms. Schneider remembered ------- a wonderful time at the company outing with her subordinates.
   (A) to having   (B) have   (C) having   (D) had

7. The company refused ------- with its competitor.
   (A) to merge   (B) merge   (C) merging   (D) having to merge

8. There is no ------- which company will enter this blue ocean.
   (A) tells   (B) tell   (C) telling   (D) told

9. Please don't fail ------- the document to the accounting department in advance.
   (A) submitting   (B) submission   (C) submit   (D) to submit

10. Due to a power failure, Graces Cosmetics stopped ------- for a day.
    (A) to operate   (B) operating   (C) operative   (D) to operating

Part 7

CheckLink **DL 101** **CD3-10**

Questions 1-5 refer to the following Web page and letter.

Home	Book	Careers	Contact Us

August 20

CHECK-IN AGENTS WANTED

McDougall Airways, five-time winner of Australia's "Excellent Service" award, is seeking hardworking, personable check-in agents for North Victoria Airport. Do you follow instructions well? Does meeting and interacting with people appeal to you? Is traveling your thing? Then, why not join our airport staff? All McDougall Airways check-in agents are required to undergo an intensive 45-hour training program. Once you pass this course, you may also apply for gate agenting and other airport jobs. Previous experience in travel-related industries is a plus, but we are willing to train promising individuals. All applicants must agree to undergo a security background check to maintain airport safety. Salary will vary depending on experience. Interested candidates are asked to submit a brief self-promoting statement as a cover letter along with a CV to Paulina Dreyfus, Human Resources, McDougall Airways, 123 Park St, Port Melbourne, VIC 5006, by September 15. Please allow seven days for a response.

Lucille Abercrombie
96 Beacon Rd
Port Melbourne, VIC 3206

September 5

Ms. Paulina Dreyfus
Human Resources
McDougall Airways
123 Park St
Port Melbourne, VIC 5006

Dear Ms. Dreyfus,

I am writing in response to your help wanted message posted on August 20. I have
worked in hospitality for Duke & Foster Down Under Cruises for ten years. Working on a
cruise ship means being involved in customer service night and day. I have had to develop
a discerning eye to anticipate issues before they happen. Advocating for passenger rights,
I was always there to make the trip as enjoyable as possible and to correct any problems
that arose. I found myself lending a helping hand whenever they needed someone to
speak with passengers. Wanting to stay closer to home with my young children and only
travel occasionally, however, I'm ready for a change. I believe I am a good candidate for
this position. I always work hard and am friendly and loyal. I am available to start right
away. The other agent opportunity also sounds good. I love learning, so the idea of an
intensive training course appeals to me.

I look forward to hearing from you at your earliest convenience.

Best regards,

Lucille Abercrombie

1. What is the purpose of the Web page?
   (A) To announce job openings at the company
   (B) To display the five service award certificates
   (C) To explain various jobs at the organization
   (D) To promote the airlines to potential passengers

2. In the Web page, the word "meeting" in line 3, is closest in meaning to
   (A) Encountering
   (B) Gathering together
   (C) Negotiating with
   (D) Reuniting

3. What is NOT a stated requirement for this position?
   (A) A willingness to work hard
   (B) An interest in communication
   (C) Having worked for an airline
   (D) Receiving some training

4. What does Ms. Abercrombie say about her work at the cruise company?
   (A) She was mostly involved in management.
   (B) She worked directly with passengers a lot.
   (C) She was in the human resources department.
   (D) She helped passengers with small children.

5. What else is Ms. Abercrombie interested in doing?
   (A) Meeting the airline president
   (B) Moving to a sister airline
   (C) Working at the gate
   (D) Working in the air

Negotiation

関係詞

Goal
- 複数の意見のやりとりがなされる場面の英文に触れ、問題の傾向を把握する
- よく出題される関係詞について整理し、頻出の応用問題を解けるようにする

 Warm-Up Questions

日本語訳を参考に、空所に入る語を (A) 〜 (D) から選びましょう。

1. 双方のニーズに合致する同意に至ることが究極の目標です。

Reaching an agreement ------- suits the needs of both parties is the ultimate goal.

(A) that　　(B) when　　(C) what　　(D) how

2. 責任者のグプタさんが、現状を説明します。

Mr. Gupta, ------- is in charge, will explain the current situation.

(A) which　　(B) when　　(C) who　　(D) how

 Words & Expressions

音声を聞いて、日本語訳に合う語を（　　）内に書き入れましょう。

1.	問題を扱う	(**h** _ _ _ _ _) the matter
2.	強い不満をもった客	a highly (**d** _ _ _ _ _ _ _ _ _ _ _) customer
3.	その分野での専門知識	(**e** _ _ _ _ _ _ _ _) in the field
4.	交渉の基本	the (**f** _ _ _ _ _ _ _ _ _ _ _) of negotiation
5.	私を手伝ってくれないでしょうか。	I was (**w** _ _ _ _ _ _ _ _) if you could help me.
6.	簡単な概要	a (**b** _ _ _ _) overview
7.	返金を求める	ask for a (**r** _ _ _ _ _)
8.	双方の同意	(**m** _ _ _ _ _) agreement
9.	その問題を話し合う	(**d** _ _ _ _ _ _) the problem
10.	会議の議長をする	(**c** _ _ _ _) the meeting
11.	対立の解決	conflict (**r** _ _ _ _ _ _ _ _ _)
12.	経験豊富な交渉者	an experienced (**n** _ _ _ _ _ _ _ _ _)
13.	話し合いをもつ	(**h** _ _ _) talks
14.	従業員に価格を再考するよう指示する	(**i** _ _ _ _ _ _ _) an employee to reconsider the price
15.	顧客に連絡する	get in (**t** _ _ _ _) with the client

91

Grammar Focus 関係詞

◎関係詞（関係代名詞・関係副詞）の先行詞と格について整理しておきましょう。

先行詞	主格	所有格	目的格
人	who / that	whose	who / whom / that
もの	which / that	whose	which / that
人＋もの	that	whose	that

◎上記以外の関係代名詞として what があります。先行詞をとらず、what SV / V「SV するもの・こと／V するもの・こと」という形で用います。

　　例：Please remember what I told you.
　　　　「私があなたに言ったことを覚えておいてください」

◎関係副詞は主語や目的語にはならず、〈接続詞＋副詞〉の機能をもちます。

　　例：We'll have a meeting tomorrow, when an important announcement will be made. 「大事な発表がある明日、私たちは会議を開きます」

◎〈前置詞＋関係詞〉や複合関係詞などの発展的事項は問題を通して学習しましょう。

 ## Practice

空所に入る語を語群から選び、文を完成させましょう。選択肢は一度しか使えません。なお、文頭に来る語も小文字で与えられています。

1. Mr. McCary will talk to those ------- might be interested in the joint project.

2. The management was impressed by ------- the customer service desk handled the matter.

3. We should listen to others and figure out what they need, ------- is the fundamentals of negotiation.

4. ------- has an opinion should feel free to let us know.

5. Floret Deco & Furniture needs to hire a person ------- expertise lies in the field of product management.

6. Imagine a case ------- customers are highly dissatisfied.

7. Ms. Lee is not convinced with the reason ------- her supervisor is sure the plan is much better.

8. The sales team will be having a brief discussion with the product development team tomorrow, ------- the matter of cost will be focused on.

9. The issue ------- we negotiate on today is highly complicated.

10. It was decided that the employees can invite ------- they like.

A. whomever	**B.** when	**C.** where	**D.** that	**E.** why
F. which	**G.** how	**H.** whose	**I.** who	**J.** whoever

🔷 Short Listening

🎧 DL 105 💿 CD3-14

次の会話を聞いて、1 ～ 4 の（　　）に語を書き入れましょう。そのあと、5 と 6 の質問に日本語で答えましょう。

M: I'm looking forward to today's lecture by Professor Helena Hopkins.

W: (1.　　　　　　　) here. She is well known for her research on business

(2.　　　　　　　　　　　), and has recently published a book on that subject.

M: Yeah, I bought that book, (3.　　　　　　) is very inspiring.

W: I heard that today's talk will focus on how to efficiently carry out a

negotiation, which I think is something (4.　　　　) our team needs to

improve upon.

---

5. ホプキンス教授は何に関する研究で有名ですか。

_____

6. 女性はチームのどのような点を改善すべきと言っていますか。

_____

🔷 Short Reading

🎧 DL 106 💿 CD3-15

次のテキスト・メッセージのやりとりを読んで、1 ～ 3 の質問に日本語で答えましょう。

Josh Larson (9:10 A.M.): I was supposed to attend today's meeting at 4:00 P.M., where I was going to speak about the development of a new product. But I was wondering if you could do it for me.

Liz Eubank (9:12 A.M.): Why? Is something wrong?

Josh Larson (9:15 A.M.): As you know, I'm in Toronto on a business trip, but my flight home has been delayed due to inclement weather. I don't think I'll be able to make it.

Liz Eubank (9:18 A.M.): Okay, I understand. The explanation for today's meeting doesn't need to be very detailed. So I'll just give them a brief overview, which I think is easy.

Josh Larson (9:19 A.M.): Thank you. That's really helpful.

---

1. ラーソンさんはもともと午後 4 時から会議で何について話す予定でしたか。

_____

2. ユーバンクさんはなぜ会議で話すことを依頼されているのですか。

_____

3. ユーバンクさんは会議で何を説明すると言っていますか。

_____

Listening

Tips! Part 1 では写真に写っている人・ものの位置関係をすばやく確認し、人が動作を行っている場合は、写真から客観的に判断できる動きは何かを考えることが大切です。Part 3 は図表を参照しつつ意見のやりとりを扱う問題に取り組みます。複数の情報が出てくるので一つ一つ整理しながら聞きましょう。

Part 1

CheckLink　DL 107　CD3-16

Look at the picture and select the statement that best describes what you see in the picture.

1.

(A)　(B)　(C)　(D)

2.

(A)　(B)　(C)　(D)

Part 3

CheckLink　DL 108　CD3-17

Listen to the conversation while looking at the graphic and select the best response to each question.

Show Time				
	Saturday		Sunday	
Title (Price)	Matinee	Evening	Matinee	Evening
Happy Days ($50)	Available	Sold Out	—	Available
Missing Man ($50)	Sold Out	Available	Sold Out	Available
Diamond Time ($85)	Sold Out	Available	—	—
Hidden Treasure ($80)	Available	Sold Out	Available	Available

1. Who most likely is the woman?

   (A) A hotel receptionist

   (B) A tour guide

   (C) An event planner

   (D) A box office clerk

2. How would it be possible for the man to get a refund?

   (A) If the performance was not canceled

   (B) If the performance was not rescheduled

   (C) If his request for a refund is made at least 24 hours prior to performance

   (D) If the tickets for the same day performance have been sold out

3. Look at the graphic. Which show will the man probably see?

   (A) Happy Days

   (B) Missing Man

   (C) Diamond Time

   (D) Hidden Treasure

Part 5

CheckLink   DL 109   CD3-18

Select the best answer to complete the sentence.

1. Both the soccer club and the player had a negotiation, ------- it was made clear that neither would move forward without mutual agreement.
   (A) when   (B) which   (C) how   (D) where

2. The R&D department decided on a location ------- was suitable for the staff to meet and discuss the problem.
   (A) that   (B) when   (C) who   (D) where

3. The negotiations ended in success, ------- pleased the client.
   (A) that   (B) how   (C) which   (D) when

4. There will surely come a time ------- both parties will agree.
   (A) which   (B) who   (C) when   (D) how

5. The three staff members, ------- the committee selected, chaired the meetings.
   (A) which   (B) why   (C) that   (D) whom

6. Conflict resolution is never an easy task, ------- is why experienced negotiators are highly sought after.
   (A) that   (B) when   (C) which   (D) what

7. The pharmaceutical giant negotiated a settlement with the opposing attorney, and ------- took several days.
   (A) which   (B) when   (C) who   (D) it

8. The developer is ready to hold talks with ------- is interested in purchasing the property.
   (A) who   (B) that   (C) whoever   (D) when

9. Bank of North will be discussing the opening of a new branch, ------- is intended to be located near the Lakewood Botanical Park.
   (A) that   (B) which   (C) why   (D) how

10. Mr. Wu, ------- contribution to his company is beyond words, will retire on May 5.
    (A) who   (B) that   (C) which   (D) whose

Part 6

CCheckLink **DL 110 ⊙CD3-19**

Questions 1-4 refer to the following notice.

May 1

To all employees:

After several years of being one of the few tenants in this big, beautiful building, several new firms will be arriving soon to fill the other floors. For this reason, we will be changing to a parking pass (magnetic-strip card) system. -------. Each week, you will receive an e-mail with this code to share with
   1.
visiting clients. In the past, you have been able to park wherever you wanted, but with all these additional cars, we ask that you park in the space that you were originally -------, i.e., the one with your name on it. -------, we would like
      2.   **3.**
to ask you to instruct your visitors to only use the spaces marked "visitor," ------- are conveniently located close to the elevator on each floor of the parking
  4.
garage. We have sent messages to those already registered explaining how to apply for special accessible parking, but anyone else who needs such a spot should get in touch with Gary Friedman in Human Resources to change parking spots.

---

1. (A) The new firms will send representatives to explain the new system to you in person.
    (B) The system will also be accessible by punching in a code that changes every week.
    (C) There are actually fewer parking spaces available on the first and second floors.
    (D) There is a list of all parking spaces online if you need to refer to it.

2. (A) assigned
    (B) decided
    (C) demanded
    (D) required

3. (A) Accordingly
    (B) Certainly
    (C) Finally
    (D) Previously

4. (A) what
    (B) where
    (C) which
    (D) whom

Unit 12 Manufacturing & Logistics
比較

Goal
・製造や流通に関する英文に触れ、よく出題されるポイントに慣れる
・比較の基本を再確認し、問題演習を通してやや発展的な項目もおさえる

 ## Warm-Up Questions　　　DL 111　CD3-20

日本語訳を参考に、空所に入る語を (A) ～ (D) から選びましょう。

1. この製品のパフォーマンスは以前のバージョンよりもすぐれています。

The performance of this product is ------- than the previous version.

(A) good　　(B) well　　(C) more　　(D) better

2. 残念ながら、我が社の製造コストはライバルほど低くはありません。

Unfortunately, our company's manufacturing costs are not ------- low as our competitors.

(A) much　　(B) less　　(C) more　　(D) as

 ## Words & Expressions　　　DL 112　CD3-21

音声を聞いて、日本語訳に合う語を（　　）内に書き入れましょう。

1. 試作品　　　　　　　　　a (p _ _ _ _ _ _ _)
2. 流通コスト　　　　　　　(d _ _ _ _ _ _ _ _ _ _) costs
3. 原材料　　　　　　　　　raw (m _ _ _ _ _ _ _)
4. 技術の進歩　　　　　　　(a _ _ _ _ _ _ _ _ _) in technology
5. 在庫管理　　　　　　　　(s _ _ _ _) management
6. 提案に反応する　　　　　respond to a (p _ _ _ _ _ _ _)
7. 開発の状況　　　　　　　the (s _ _ _ _ _) of development
8. プロセスを合理化する　　(s _ _ _ _ _ _ _ _) the process
9. 欠陥品　　　　　　　　　a (d _ _ _ _ _ _ _) product
10. 汚れた部品　　　　　　　a (c _ _ _ _ _ _ _ _ _ _) part
11. ジョイントを検査する　　(i _ _ _ _ _ _) the joint
12. はっきり見えるヒビ　　　(v _ _ _ _ _) cracks
13. 機器を輸送する　　　　　(t _ _ _ _ _ _ _ _) the equipment
14. 保管プロセスの最適化　　(o _ _ _ _ _ _ _ _ _ _ _) of storage processes
15. 倉庫の管理　　　　　　　(w _ _ _ _ _ _ _ _) management

98

Grammar Focus 比較

比較を用いた表現は TOEIC L&R では最頻出事項の一つです。まず、基本をおさらいしましょう。

(1) 同等比較

as ... as で比較したいポイントを挟みます。

例：Mr. Harris works **as hard as** Mr. Jensen.

(2) 比較

形容詞や副詞に -er、あるいは more（程度が劣る場合は less）を付けて表現します。

例：Ms. Price's response to the e-mail was **quicker than** mine.

The engine runs **more strongly than** the previous one.

(3) 最上級

形容詞や副詞に -est、あるいは most を付けて表現します。

例：Ms. Richards works **hardest** in this company.

This is **the most wonderful** experience that I have ever had.

個別の語法や表現については問題を通して確認をしていきましょう。

 Practice

DL 113 CD3-22

空所に入る語句を語群から選び、文を完成させましょう。選択肢は一度しか使えません。

1. As A&P IT has increased their IT department staff now, they are able to develop product designs faster than they -------.

2. The manufacturer successfully created a ------- efficient supply chain than they had previously by linking raw material suppliers and distributors.

3. With the advancement of AI technology, moving materials between production lines has become faster and ------- troublesome.

4. Please take advantage of our logistics system, which is the fastest we have ------- established.

5. In industrial logistics, stock management is one of the ------- fundamental things for achieving faster production.

6. As ------- as 100 people provided feedback on the prototype.

7. We are confident that the quality of this new product is the ------- best one we've ever achieved.

8. Columbus Appliance's new production system is ------- as efficient as their old one.

9. The ------- you respond to this proposal, the better for me.

10. To achieve cost efficiency, ------- firms are turning to local suppliers.

A. more and more	**B.** ever	**C.** less	**D.** many	**E.** sooner
F. used to	**G.** very	**H.** twice	**I.** most	**J.** more

 **Short Listening**

🎧 DL 114　◎ CD3-23

次の電話のメッセージを聞いて、1〜4の（　　）に語を書き入れましょう。そのあと、5と6の質問に日本語で答えましょう。

> **M:** Hi, this is Roy Turner from the Production (¹.　　　　　　　　). As I
> mentioned in my e-mail, I still have not (².　　　　　　) the parts for the
> dishwasher, and I have not heard anything. Do you know the (³.　　　　　)
> of my request? Please check and get (⁴.　　　　) to me as soon as possible.
> We are in a hurry as we need to finish assembling the dishwasher and get it
> shipped within 10 days.

5. ターナーさんの所属部署は何ですか。

_____

6. どのような問題が生じていますか。

_____

🔷 Short Reading

🎧 DL 115　◎ CD3-24

次の記事を読んで、1〜3の質問に日本語で答えましょう。

> Over the past two years, MG Express has thoroughly streamlined its distribution
> system and established one of the fastest distribution processes in the industry. As a
> result, the company is gaining more and more profits. How was this made possible?
> To learn more about how MG Express has accomplished this, read the interview
> with their president that will be appearing in next month's *Logistic Matters*.

1. MG エクスプレス社は過去2年間で何を行いましたか。

_____

2. MG エクスプレス社が過去2年間に行ったことにより、どのような結果が生じましたか。

3. 書き手は読者に何を勧めていますか。

_____

TOEIC Practice

Listening

Part 2, 4

Tips! Part 2 で比較が出題される場合、当然のことですが何と何が比較されているのかをよく把握することが重要です。文脈によっては比較表現以外のものが正答になることもあります。その文脈で一番自然なやりとりは何かということを考えましょう。Part 4 はクレームもよく出題されます。どのような問題があって、どのような解決策を求めているのかという点に集中しましょう。

Part 2

CheckLink DL 116 CD3-25

Listen to the question or statement and the three responses. Then select the best response to each question or statement.

1. (A)　　(B)　　(C)

2. (A)　　(B)　　(C)

3. (A)　　(B)　　(C)

Part 4

CheckLink DL 117 CD3-26

Listen to the talk and select the best response to each question.

1. What can be said about past shipments of welded joint pipes?

(A) They were better than the ones just received.

(B) The joint pipes were mostly defective.

(C) The parts received had visible defects.

(D) Their base metal may have been contaminated.

2. What has been separated?

(A) Joint pipes without cracks but of lower quality

(B) Joint pipes that can be used and those that cannot

(C) Units just received and those previously shipped

(D) Units that were poorly welded and joint pipes with cracks

3. What will the speaker probably do after leaving this message?

(A) Visit a construction site

(B) Inspect the joint pipes for defects

(C) Receive a new shipment of joint pipes

(D) Send back the defective joint pipes

Tips! ▶ Part 5 では、比較表現の発展的な知識も問われますが、基本に立ち返って、原級・比較級・最上級のどれが文法的にふさわしいかという点で解いてみましょう。Part 7 では、チャット問題に挑戦します。読解問題としてよりは、チャットに参加しているつもりで取り組んでみましょう。

Part 5

CheckLink 🎧 DL 118 ⊙ CD3-27

Select the best answer to complete the sentence.

1. The new distribution control system will allow us to ship goods as efficiently ------- before, but at a lower cost.
   (A) than   (B) as   (C) more   (D) better

2. Production has been flowing ------- in recent times.
   (A) faster than   (B) faster   (C) as fast as   (D) no faster than

3. Raw materials are more difficult to transport in winter -------.
   (A) than during summer   (C) as well as summer
   (B) than summer   (D) less than summer

4. Many industrial firms in the country are sourcing ------- materials from China.
   (A) cheapest   (B) as cheap as   (C) cheaper   (D) cheaper than

5. The production plants in California are ------- bigger than what we have in Texas.
   (A) as   (B) much   (C) more   (D) most

6. The optimization of storage processes is more expensive today than ------- ten years ago.
   (A) it   (B) it is   (C) it was   (D) it has been

7. The automation of material transportation has led to ------- accidents.
   (A) much   (B) lesser   (C) little   (D) fewer

8. We are proud that our warehouse management system is better than ------- you can find anywhere else.
   (A) things   (B) some   (C) other   (D) anything

9. Please contact the distribution department at your -------.
   (A) most convenient   (C) convenient
   (B) earliest convenience   (D) more convenient

10. The materials requested from the warehouse arrived faster than Mr. Nelson -------.
    (A) expect   (B) expects   (C) expectation   (D) had expected

Part 7

CheckLink   DL 119   CD3-28

Questions 1-4 refer to the following online chat discussion.

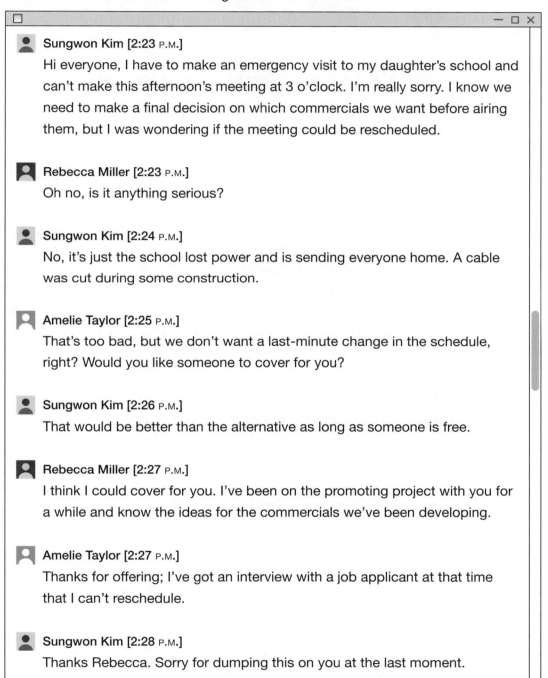

Sungwon Kim [2:23 P.M.]

Hi everyone, I have to make an emergency visit to my daughter's school and can't make this afternoon's meeting at 3 o'clock. I'm really sorry. I know we need to make a final decision on which commercials we want before airing them, but I was wondering if the meeting could be rescheduled.

Rebecca Miller [2:23 P.M.]

Oh no, is it anything serious?

Sungwon Kim [2:24 P.M.]

No, it's just the school lost power and is sending everyone home. A cable was cut during some construction.

Amelie Taylor [2:25 P.M.]

That's too bad, but we don't want a last-minute change in the schedule, right? Would you like someone to cover for you?

Sungwon Kim [2:26 P.M.]

That would be better than the alternative as long as someone is free.

Rebecca Miller [2:27 P.M.]

I think I could cover for you. I've been on the promoting project with you for a while and know the ideas for the commercials we've been developing.

Amelie Taylor [2:27 P.M.]

Thanks for offering; I've got an interview with a job applicant at that time that I can't reschedule.

Sungwon Kim [2:28 P.M.]

Thanks Rebecca. Sorry for dumping this on you at the last moment.

1. Why does Mr. Kim have to pick up his child from school?
   (A) She finished early.
   (B) His wife couldn't go.
   (C) She became sick.
   (D) The school is shutting down.

2. What department are Mr. Kim and Ms. Miller inferred to be working in?
   (A) Marketing
   (B) Legal
   (C) Finance
   (D) Construction

3. Why can't Ms. Taylor go to the meeting?
   (A) She has to pick up her own child from school.
   (B) She does not know enough about the meeting.
   (C) She will be working on hiring a new employee.
   (D) She will be teaching a class at that time.

4. At 2:26 P.M., what does Mr. Kim mean when he writes "That would be better than the alternative"?
   (A) It would be better if someone went to the meeting in his place.
   (B) It would be better if the meeting was scheduled for another time.
   (C) It would be better if someone else picked up his child.
   (D) It would be better if he presented the commercial ideas himself.

Unit 13 Finance

仮定法

Goal
・お金やそのやりとりに関する英文を読めるようになる
・仮定法の頻出事項の理解を徹底し、英文理解に役立てることができる

Warm-Up Questions ⬇ DL 120 ◉ CD3-29

日本語訳を参考に、空所に入る語を (A) ～ (D) から選びましょう。

1. もっと予算があれば、製品を速く作ることができるのに。

If we ------- a larger budget, we could develop our products faster.

(A) have (B) had (C) have had (D) had had

2. マッキンリーさんは期限内に領収書を提出していれば、旅行の返金がされていただろうに。

Mr. McKinley ------- reimbursed for the trip if he had submitted his receipts in time.

(A) have been (B) would be (C) had been (D) would have been

Words & Expressions ⬇ DL 121 ◉ CD3-30

音声を聞いて、日本語訳に合う語を（　　）内に書き入れましょう。

1. 製造費を削減する　　　　　　cut costs on (**p** _ _ _ _ _ _ _ _ _)

2. 2つ目の案を採用する　　　　(**a** _ _ _ _) the second plan

3. 収益を生み出す　　　　　　　(**g** _ _ _ _ _ _ _) revenue

4. セールに参加する　　　　　　(**p** _ _ _ _ _ _ _ _ _ _) in the sale

5. スマートフォンを発売する　　(**r** _ _ _ _ _ _) a smartphone

6. 経営に関して　　　　　　　　regarding (**m** _ _ _ _ _ _ _ _ _)

7. コスト削減　　　　　　　　　cost (**r** _ _ _ _ _ _ _ _)

8. 価格帯　　　　　　　　　　　price (**r** _ _ _ _)

9. 請求書を確認する　　　　　　take a look at the (**i** _ _ _ _ _ _)

10. 多く課金される　　　　　　　be (**o** _ _ _ _ _ _ _ _ _ _)

11. 費用効率　　　　　　　　　　cost (**e** _ _ _ _ _ _ _ _ _)

12. お得な値段で　　　　　　　　at a (**r** _ _ _ _ _ _ _ _ _) price

13. 必要以上に　　　　　　　　　more than (**n** _ _ _ _ _ _ _ _)

14. 延長された保証期間　　　　　extended (**w** _ _ _ _ _ _ _)

15. 割引の資格がある　　　　　　be (**e** _ _ _ _ _ _ _) for a discount

105

Grammar Focus 仮定法

仮定法は現実ではないことを仮定的に述べる際に用います。まずは基本の形を確認しましょう。

仮定法過去 [現在の非現実]	If ＋主語＋動詞の過去形,	主語＋助動詞の過去形＋動詞の原形
	If I had time, If I were you,	I would come with you. I would first call customer service.
仮定法過去完了 [過去の非現実]	If ＋主語＋ had ＋過去分詞,	主語＋助動詞の過去形＋ have ＋過去分詞
	If I'd known about your party, If you had not helped us,	I would have come. this project would not have been successful.

これらの基本の形をおさえた上で、以下の重要表現も確認しましょう。

・I wish / If only ＋仮定法「～ならよいのに／～でありさえすればなあ」

　※ 現在のことを言うときは仮定法過去を、過去のことを言うときは仮定法過去完了を用いる

他の用法などについては問題を通して学習しましょう。

 **Practice**

空所に入る語句を語群から選び、文を完成させましょう。選択肢は一度しか使えません。なお、文頭に来る語も小文字で与えられています。

1. If the budget ------- limited, this project would not have been possible.
2. If they hadn't hired Ms. Anderson at that time, the company ------- able to generate so much revenue.
3. I wish I ------- that coupon code now.
4. Management demanded that we ------- cut costs on our production.
5. If I ------- you, I would adopt the second plan.
6. By participating in our online sale, you can enjoy shopping as ------- you were shopping in a real store.
7. ------- your advice, I would have bought the coat before the sale.
8. Without her meticulous planning, this project ------- be possible on such a low budget.
9. ------- we could invest more in the AI industry.
10. I wish I ------- that portable charger during that year-end sale.

A. had been   **B.** had   **C.** if only   **D.** were   **E.** if
F. had it not been for   **G.** would not   **H.** should   **I.** had bought
J. wouldn't have been

106

 Short Listening

DL 123　CD3-32

次の会話を聞いて、1〜4の（　　）に語を書き入れましょう。そのあと、5と6の質問に日本語で答えましょう。

M: Have you bought SmartTech's new smartphone that was (1.　　　　　　　)
　　a month ago?

W: Yes, I've already got one. I like the latest features very much.

M: I also bought one, but there is one thing I (2.　　　　　　).

W: What's that?

M: This smartphone is going to be sold at a (3.　　　　　　) for two days
　　starting tomorrow.

W: What? I wish I (4.　　　　) known that earlier, too.

5. 女性は新しいスマートフォンの何を気に入っていますか。

_____

6. スマートフォンのセールは2人にとってなぜ問題なのですか。

_____

Short Reading

DL 124　CD3-33

次の手紙を読んで、1〜3の質問に日本語で答えましょう。

Dear Dr. Higgins,

Thank you very much for the advice you gave us last year regarding the management of
our company. We followed your advice and carefully reviewed our business plan, and we
were able to achieve a significant reduction in costs. If we had not consulted you at that
time, we would not have been able to achieve such success.

1. ヒギンズさんの職業はおそらく何ですか。

_____

2. この会社はヒギンズさんから助言をもらったあと、何をしましたか。

_____

3. この会社は何を成し遂げることができましたか。

_____

Listening

> **Tips!** Part 1 では再度、位置関係を意識してみましょう。写真全体を見て構図をすばやく確認してください。Part 3 は会話の場面に実際に参加しているつもりで聞きましょう。数字にも要注意です。

Part 1

CheckLink DL 125 CD3-34

Look at the picture and select the statement that best describes what you see in the picture.

1.

(A) (B) (C) (D)

2.

(A) (B) (C) (D)

Part 3

CheckLink DL 126 CD3-35

Listen to the conversation and select the best response to each question.

1. Where is this conversation probably taking place?
   (A) At a college
   (B) At an electronics store
   (C) In the woman's house
   (D) In a teacher's office

2. What type of computer is recommended?
   (A) A computer with a big screen that can be taken to classes
   (B) A computer that is in the $600 to $700 price range
   (C) A computer with less memory and pre-installed software
   (D) A computer with enough memory but less software

3. What will probably happen next?
   (A) The mother and son will compare laptop computers.
   (B) The mother will take her son to college with a computer.
   (C) The mother will buy her son the cheapest computer.
   (D) Software will be installed on a laptop computer.

Reading

Tips! Part 5 では、仮定法の基本形のほか、倒置などにも注意して選択肢を吟味してください。Part 7 では、書き手は仮定法を用いて何を伝えようとしているのか、現実はどうなのかなどを考えながら文章を読みましょう。

Part 5

CheckLink DL 127 CD3-36

Select the best answer to complete the sentence.

1. Mr. Martinez suggested that his colleagues ------- a look at the invoice to make sure they are not being overcharged.
   (A) take   (B) to take   (C) taking   (D) can take

2. If you ------- have any question regarding the budget, please contact us anytime.
   (A) would   (B) should   (C) could   (D) had

3. If the release date ------- earlier, this product would get more attention.
   (A) am   (B) will be   (C) were   (D) has been

4. Lev Inc. ------- cut down on the costs if they had decided to streamline the process.
   (A) will   (B) could have   (C) should   (D) were able to

5. It is imperative that each staff member ------- always aware of cost efficiency.
   (A) are   (B) to be   (C) will be   (D) be

6. If Ms. Grant had the discount coupon, she ------- buy the mower for 50% off.
   (A) can   (B) could   (C) am able to   (D) could have

7. Mr. Brown, the CEO of SanNet, wishes that his company ------- more in AI technology ventures.
   (A) is invested   (B) invests   (C) had invested   (D) will invest

8. Given that installing new equipment ------- then, Mr. Phillips is happy that his unit was repaired at a reasonable price.
   (A) is costly   (C) had been costly
   (B) will be costly   (D) would have been costly

9. That project could not have been this profitable ------- Ms. Takada's dedication.
   (A) instead of   (B) not for   (C) without   (D) regardless

10. The accounting department would have paid more than necessary ------- the miscalculation.
    (A) had they overlooked   (C) they overlooked
    (B) they had overlooked   (D) did they overlook

Part 7

Questions 1-5 refer to the following advertisement and e-mails.

BARVILLE TECH SUNDAY SUPER SALE FOR PREMIUM MEMBERS

This Sunday, get all the tech you need at the best prices of the year!

Come to the site starting at 8 A.M. Pacific Time (11 A.M. Eastern) to "spin" our bonus wheel and unlock extra savings codes for $5, $10, and $20 off of Sunday's *purchase. (One spin per customer, ends at 11 P.M. Pacific Time.)*

Save 50% on flat screen TVs and monitors!
Save 30% on computers, notebooks, and tablets!
Free extended warranties on all products!*

We recommend that each of our Premium members enroll now in the Refer-a-Friend Program (click here) and take this opportunity to introduce friends to our Premium Program. Premium members will receive triple bonus points on every purchase a friend makes from now to the end of this month.

*The length of the extended warranty varies from product to product. It is imperative that the buyer register the product immediately to be eligible for the extended warranty program.

To:	sales@barvilletech.com
From:	Philip Seligman <pseligman@seligmanfam.com>
Date:	September 5
Subject:	Premium Member Questions

Dear Barville Tech,

I recently became a Premium member. I actually referred a friend on September 1 who purchased a flat screen TV. I have two questions about this. Your announcement went up on September 3. My friend purchased a flat screen TV on September 2. Will I still be eligible for the bonus points? Actually, if I had been aware of the sale, I would have told my friend to wait and be eligible for your big discounts. I find this extremely disappointing. I know you are trying to get Premium members to introduce new customers, and that is exactly what I did. Is there anything you can do for him, Greg Rifkin, in light of the circumstances?

Sincerely,

Philip Seligman

To: Philip Seligman <pseligman@seligmanfam.com>

From: sales@barvilletech.com

Date: September 7

Subject: Re: Premium Member Questions

Dear Phil,

Thank you for contacting us at Barville Tech.

Our Sunday Super Sale is a kind of "flash" sale, so we only announce it a few days before. I wish it were possible to let our Premium members know a few days earlier, but our marketing department has their schedule. Your friend became a Premium member, so I have credited your friend with the equivalent of $150 in points/store credit. If he had bought the same item during the sale, he would have saved slightly less than this amount, so this is actually an extra little bonus. This means, of course, he has to make another purchase, but these points do not expire, so he can use them any time he is interested in shopping with us. I have also sent Mr. Rifkin the paperwork for a free extended warranty on his purchase. As for your bonus points, I have credited your account with three times the usual points based on the $350 your friend spent.

If there is any other way I can be of service, please contact me or Carol Kaufman at sales2@barvilletech.com.

Yours sincerely,

Karen S. Mayfield
Customer Service
Barville Tech

1. What kind of business is Barville Tech?
   (A) A software company
   (B) An internet provider
   (C) An electronics seller
   (D) A premium phone provider

2. What does Mr. Seligman mention as a problem?
   (A) He forgot to enter his Premium number when he last shopped.
   (B) He has not received the item he ordered on the Web site.
   (C) He introduced a friend before the promotion was announced.
   (D) He was introduced by a friend, but the friend got no credit.

3. What was the $350 purchase for?
   (A) A computer
   (B) A monitor
   (C) A tablet
   (D) A television

4. Who authorized the gift of $150 Barville Tech credit?
   (A) Mr. Rifkin
   (B) Mr. Seligman
   (C) Ms. Kaufman
   (D) Ms. Mayfield

5. What has Mr. Rifkin received from the company?
   (A) A replacement TV
   (B) A membership for his friend and bonus points
   (C) An extended warranty and extra points
   (D) Three times the usual bonus points

Review Test 2

Listening

Part 1

↻CheckLink ⬇DL 129 ⊙CD3-38

Look at the picture and select the statement that best describes what you see in the picture.

1.

(A) (B) (C) (D)

2.

(A) (B) (C) (D)

Part 2

↻CheckLink ⬇DL 130 ⊙CD3-39

Listen to the question or statement and the three responses. Then select the best response to each question or statement.

3. (A) (B) (C)
4. (A) (B) (C)
5. (A) (B) (C)
6. (A) (B) (C)
7. (A) (B) (C)
8. (A) (B) (C)

Part 3

Listen to the conversations and select the best response to each question.

9. What decision should management make soon?
   (A) How to rename the company after the merger
   (B) Which drinks to promote for the company image
   (C) When to launch drink tests in various markets
   (D) How to boost sales in the Pacific Northwest market

10. What does the man mean when he says, "the reverse is also true"?
   (A) Products well known in the Pacific Northwest aren't known in the Southwest.
   (B) Southwest Drinks managers aren't well-known in the Pacific Northwest.
   (C) Western Beverages products are not well-known in either region yet.
   (D) Testing data established that their drinks were well-known in both regions.

11. What will the woman probably do in the afternoon?
   (A) Recommend a drink as the company's flagship product
   (B) Promote new products in markets in the Pacific Northwest
   (C) Suggest the company become more competitive in the Southwest
   (D) Tell her client's management about the idea of testing products in particular markets

⟳CheckLink DL 132 ⊙CD3-41

Factory Production and Staff Information			
Factory	Employees	Distance from main factory	Work Hours per week
Bakersfield	180	3hrs	7,200
Fresno	130	4hrs	5,200
Oxnard	160	30mins	6,400
Ventura (Main)	150		6,000

12. Why hasn't the legal department finished writing the contract?

(A) The customer wants costs to be reduced.

(B) The production department needs to increase output.

(C) Mr. Stevens hasn't agreed to the changes.

(D) The client wanted an earlier delivery date.

13. What does the woman mean when she says, "No, that wasn't it"?

(A) The shipping cost was not the problem.

(B) The delivery was too slow.

(C) Production was not the client's concern.

(D) The quality of goods was not up to standard.

14. Look at the graphic. From which factory will workers most likely be transferred?

(A) The Bakersfield factory

(B) The Fresno factory

(C) The Oxnard factory

(D) The Ventura factory

Listen to the talks and select the best response to each question.

15. What will happen at the company tomorrow?

(A) A newly remodeled employee cafeteria will open.

(B) Company employees will be requested to eat healthier.

(C) New employees will be invited to a reception in the cafeteria.

(D) The newly renovated cafeteria will be open 24 hours a day.

16. Why were changes to the cafeteria made?

(A) The company wanted to reduce unnecessary costs.

(B) The old cafeteria was unsafe for employees.

(C) Employees requested changes.

(D) Employees will be able to work longer hours.

17. Who may eat at the cafeteria for free starting tomorrow?

(A) Only full-time employees

(B) Full-time employees and clients

(C) Both part-time and full-time employees

(D) Part-time employees working overtime

CheckLink   DL 134   CD3-43

Routes (Eastville to:)	Chester	Aston	Millstone	Whitebridge
Usual driving time	8hrs	8.5hrs	9hrs	10.5hrs
Weather forecast for 2/14 (Fri)				

18. Why was the announcement made at this time?

(A) It was the first order of business of the new fiscal year.

(B) Dispatchers will have their work hours reduced from February.

(C) The government introduced a new law regarding truck drivers.

(D) Poor weather is expected to occur starting in February.

19. According to the speaker, what effects can poor weather have?

(A) Make driving more dangerous

(B) Add to fuel costs

(C) Decrease visibility on roads

(D) Increase driving time for drivers

20. Look at the graphic. For weekday drivers who have already logged 40 hours for a week, which is the best route they should take on February 14?

(A) Eastville to Chester

(B) Eastville to Aston

(C) Eastville to Millstone

(D) Eastville to Whitebridge

Reading

Part 5

CheckLink   DL 135   CD3-44

Select the best answer to complete the sentence.

21. In this training course, employees will learn what it is like ------- with customers.

(A) deals   (B) to deal   (C) to dealing   (D) deal

22. Mr. Kaminski, ------- commitment to his work has made him a role model for other employees, will be retiring next month.

(A) who   (B) whose   (C) his   (D) of him

23. The latest model of our translation machines performs ------- better than the one launched by one of our competitors last month.

(A) very   (B) much   (C) more   (D) lot

24. If the plane had been delayed, Ms. Kobayashi ------- in Tokyo now.

(A) would not be   (B) would not have been   (C) will not   (D) am not

25. Don't ------- our Web site for discount information to make sure you are getting the best value for your money.

(A) remember checking   (C) forget checking

(B) remember to check   (D) forget to check

26. ------- orders will be processed for shipping immediately.

(A) Confirm   (B) Confirming   (C) Confirmed   (D) Confirmation

27. At the next meeting, we will discuss ------- the new product's list price lower than originally planned.

(A) make   (B) made   (C) to make   (D) making

28. As ------- as 300 people came to TKT's new product launch.

(A) far   (B) many   (C) much   (D) soon

Part 6

CheckLink DL 136 CD3-45

Questions 29-32 refer to the following letter.

Wright Time Watches and Clocks

19875 Drury Ave.

Richmond, VA 23223

April 15

Mr. Robert Hobson

1458 Cherry Lane

Hennepin, MN 55416

Dear Mr. Hobson,

We wish to apologize. Under ordinary circumstances, you should have already

received the smartwatch you ordered on April 1, but currently all of our deliveries

are behind schedule. ------- the highest standards with our timepieces is a source
        29.

of pride. It is imperative that every watch ------- rigorous inspections before
                                   30.

leaving our facility. Due to circumstances beyond our control, we are rather

understaffed. -------, we ask for your understanding as the inspection process
        31.

may take some time. We keep a running account of all of our inventory. -------.
                                                          32.

The item should reach you no later than April 30.

Sincerely,

Janet Wright Gilmore

---

29. (A) Maintain
    (B) Maintained
    (C) Maintaining
    (D) Maintains

30. (A) did undergo
    (B) had undergone
    (C) undergo
    (D) underwent

31. (A) Therefore
    (B) Conversely
    (C) However
    (D) Similarly

32. (A) Accordingly, your watch will arrive at our dispatch center on April 23.
    (B) Consequently, the refund you have requested will be processed by April 25.
    (C) Nonetheless, management will review your feedback from April 10.
    (D) Unfortunately, you are not eligible for an upgrade until April of next year.

Part 7

Questions 33-35 refer to the following advertisement.

A Boutique Experience in Scenic Waikiki!

Welcome to Hoku Makai, a new, 50-suite boutique hotel in Waikiki. Hoku Makai, our low-rise, three-story property, opens on February 1. Make a reservation before January 15 and receive the Early-bird Rate of just $129 per night. Enjoy a maximum of four nights at this great rate. Best of all, parking is free! (Click here to book.)

Forget those tall buildings. You may be used to staying in sprawling resorts, but this will definitely be a more intimate, friendlier experience. If you want to really feel like you are in Hawaii, stay at the smaller, cozier Hoku Makai. All guests will be treated to ultimate comfort in a private suite, fabulous service, an HM welcome basket, and our terrific "garden pool." Swim in the pool in our lovely Hawaiian garden, or you may want to take the five-minute walk to world-famous Waikiki Beach.

Superb accommodations and a gracious atmosphere make this one of the most exciting new properties to open in years. We believe you'll want to return time and time again. We are right next door, and have a connecting entrance, to Aloha Java, one of the most exciting cafés in the greater Honolulu area. People come from all around the island to enjoy the wonderful drinks and light, healthy meals that give this restaurant its 5-star online rating. Go to hokumakaihotel.com/coupon to get 10% off your next meal at Aloha Java.

Opening rates are valid Monday through Thursday only (through May 30) and do not include tax (14%). Unless you are a Hawaii resident, there is also a resort tax of $10 a day; however, this is the lowest rate among resort hotels. Weekend rates are available (they are slightly higher). Reservations are based on availability. Pre-payment using a major credit card is required to guarantee your reservation.

33. What is the main purpose of this ad?

    (A) To advertise a new hotel in Waikiki

    (B) To explain the hotel's policy on parking

    (C) To introduce a group of Waikiki hotels

    (D) To promote both hotel rates and Honolulu

34. What is the longest length of stay possible at the $129 rate?

    (A) Any length of stay until May 30

    (B) Four nights that must include a weekend

    (C) Four nights, not including weekends

    (D) From now until the end of this year

35. What benefit is only for people who live in Hawaii?

    (A) They don't have to pay the parking fee.

    (B) They will get daily coupons to Aloha Java.

    (C) They will receive the HM welcome basket.

    (D) They won't have the added resort fee.

Questions 36-40 refer to the following Web site and e-mails.

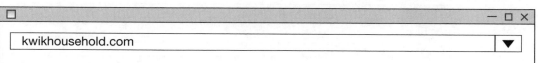

kwikhousehold.com

Kwik Household Online Shopping

Shopping Cart Summary
Date: July 9
Order #: 00098764327
Customer: Jayne Sanchez
3986 Meadowbrook Rd.
Elwood, KS 66024

Item	Quantity	Charge
Organic Tomato Soup 3-packs	1	$10.50
Paper Towels 6-rolls	1	$6
Organic White Beans 4-packs	1	$9
Case Brightwell Spring Water 4 1-liter bottles	1	$15.12

Sub Total : $40.62
Tax (Kansas) : $2.64
Shipping : $0.00
Total : $43.26

kwikhousehold.com, the better online shopping experience—more choices, more savings.
Your one-stop shop for household cleaning items, dry (canned, packaged) foods, etc. We have it all!

- All orders over $40 get free shipping.
- Kwik Household collects tax according to each state's laws.
- Your credit card will not be charged until the item ships.
- To reorder from a former purchase, click here.

From:	orders@kwikhousehold.com (do not reply)
To:	Jayne Sanchez <jsanchez@ks.tt.com>
Date:	July 11
Subject:	Invoice / Receipt

Dear Jayne Sanchez,

Order #: 00098764327
Order Date: 7/9
Shipping Date: 7/11
Amount: $43.26
Status: Paid
Credit Card: xxxx xxxx xxxx 8103

Thank you for shopping with Kwik Household.

For questions or issues, feel free to contact Customer Service:
info@kwikhousehold.com
Or call: 888-555-3200

From:	Jayne Sanchez <jsanchez@ks.tt.com>
To:	info@kwikhousehold.com
Date:	July 17
Subject:	Invoice Issue

Dear Customer Service,

On July 11, you shipped my order 00098764327. Inside the box was a note that the paper towels were out of stock and you were unsure when/if you would be getting them back. Unfortunately, you charged me for this item. I have checked my credit card statement online, and I see the full charge of $43.26. This goes against your policy, as stated on the shopping cart page. I would like you either to refund the amount of the missing item (plus tax) immediately, or ship me a pack of the same size in another brand. To make matters worse, I tried to call your Customer Service line, but it would only let me leave a message. I left two messages asking for someone to call me back, and that did not happen. I hope you will resolve this issue right away.

Sincerely,

Jayne Sanchez

36. What kind of business is Kwik Household?

(A) Home design

(B) House cleaning

(C) Property sales

(D) Internet shopping

37. What does the e-mail from the store imply about the status of Ms. Sanchez's order?

(A) Ms. Sanchez forgot to enter her credit card.

(B) Ms. Sanchez needs to get online and pay.

(C) The order has been shipped and paid for.

(D) The order will be filled in a few days.

38. What happened when Ms. Sanchez called the company?

(A) She got no response.

(B) She was told to e-mail them instead.

(C) They canceled her order by mistake.

(D) They sent her a promotional coupon.

39. How much is the item Ms. Sanchez mentions in her e-mail?

(A) $6

(B) $9

(C) $10.50

(D) $15.12

40. Which part of Shopping Cart Summary statement does Ms. Sanchez imply was not followed?

(A) They charge state tax in some states.

(B) They do not add shipping fees on orders over $40.

(C) They do not charge the credit card until items are sent.

(D) They have many different products.

このシールをはがすと
CheckLink 利用のための
「**教科書固有番号**」が
記載されています。

一度はがすと元に戻すことは
できませんのでご注意下さい。

◀ ここからはがして下さい

4155
BASIC UNDERSTANDING
(TOEIC)

CheckLink

本書にはCD（別売）があります

BASIC UNDERSTANDING OF THE TOEIC® L&R TEST
TOEIC® L&Rテスト基礎徹底トレーニング

2022年1月20日　初版第1刷発行
2024年2月20日　初版第4刷発行

著　者　　小倉　雅明

発行者　　福岡　正人
発行所　　株式会社　金星堂

（〒101-0051）　東京都千代田区神田神保町 3-21
Tel　　（03）3263-3828（営業部）
　　　　（03）3263-3997（編集部）
Fax　　（03）3263-0716
https://www.kinsei-do.co.jp

編集担当　池田恭子・長島吉成　　　　　　　　　　　Printed in Japan
印刷所・製本所／萩原印刷株式会社

ISBN978-4-7647-4155-3　C1082

Review Test 1　マークシート

学籍番号	
ふりがな	
名　前	

LISTENING SECTION

Part 1

No.	ANSWER			
	A	B	C	D
1	Ⓐ	Ⓑ	Ⓒ	Ⓓ
2	Ⓐ	Ⓑ	Ⓒ	Ⓓ

Part 2

No.	ANSWER		
	A	B	C
3	Ⓐ	Ⓑ	Ⓒ
4	Ⓐ	Ⓑ	Ⓒ
5	Ⓐ	Ⓑ	Ⓒ
6	Ⓐ	Ⓑ	Ⓒ

Part 3

No.	ANSWER			
	A	B	C	D
7	Ⓐ	Ⓑ	Ⓒ	
8	Ⓐ	Ⓑ	Ⓒ	

No.	ANSWER			
	A	B	C	D
9	Ⓐ	Ⓑ	Ⓒ	Ⓓ
10	Ⓐ	Ⓑ	Ⓒ	Ⓓ
11	Ⓐ	Ⓑ	Ⓒ	Ⓓ
12	Ⓐ	Ⓑ	Ⓒ	Ⓓ

Part 4

No.	ANSWER			
	A	B	C	D
13	Ⓐ	Ⓑ	Ⓒ	Ⓓ
14	Ⓐ	Ⓑ	Ⓒ	Ⓓ

No.	ANSWER			
	A	B	C	D
15	Ⓐ	Ⓑ	Ⓒ	Ⓓ
16	Ⓐ	Ⓑ	Ⓒ	Ⓓ
17	Ⓐ	Ⓑ	Ⓒ	Ⓓ
18	Ⓐ	Ⓑ	Ⓒ	Ⓓ

No.	ANSWER			
	A	B	C	D
19	Ⓐ	Ⓑ	Ⓒ	Ⓓ
20	Ⓐ	Ⓑ	Ⓒ	Ⓓ

READING SECTION

Part 5

No.	ANSWER			
	A	B	C	D
21	Ⓐ	Ⓑ	Ⓒ	Ⓓ
22	Ⓐ	Ⓑ	Ⓒ	Ⓓ
23	Ⓐ	Ⓑ	Ⓒ	Ⓓ
24	Ⓐ	Ⓑ	Ⓒ	Ⓓ

Part 6

No.	ANSWER			
	A	B	C	D
25	Ⓐ	Ⓑ	Ⓒ	Ⓓ
26	Ⓐ	Ⓑ	Ⓒ	Ⓓ
27	Ⓐ	Ⓑ	Ⓒ	Ⓓ
28	Ⓐ	Ⓑ	Ⓒ	Ⓓ

No.	ANSWER			
	A	B	C	D
29	Ⓐ	Ⓑ	Ⓒ	Ⓓ
30	Ⓐ	Ⓑ	Ⓒ	Ⓓ
31	Ⓐ	Ⓑ	Ⓒ	Ⓓ
32	Ⓐ	Ⓑ	Ⓒ	Ⓓ

Part 7

No.	ANSWER			
	A	B	C	D
33	Ⓐ	Ⓑ	Ⓒ	Ⓓ
34	Ⓐ	Ⓑ	Ⓒ	Ⓓ
35	Ⓐ	Ⓑ	Ⓒ	Ⓓ
36	Ⓐ	Ⓑ	Ⓒ	Ⓓ

No.	ANSWER			
	A	B	C	D
37	Ⓐ	Ⓑ	Ⓒ	Ⓓ
38	Ⓐ	Ⓑ	Ⓒ	Ⓓ
39	Ⓐ	Ⓑ	Ⓒ	Ⓓ
40	Ⓐ	Ⓑ	Ⓒ	Ⓓ

Review Test 2　マークシート

学籍番号	
ふりがな	
名　前	

LISTENING SECTION

Part 1

No.	ANSWER A B C D
1	Ⓐ Ⓑ Ⓒ Ⓓ
2	Ⓐ Ⓑ Ⓒ Ⓓ

Part 2

No.	ANSWER A B C
3	Ⓐ Ⓑ Ⓒ
4	Ⓐ Ⓑ Ⓒ
5	Ⓐ Ⓑ Ⓒ
6	Ⓐ Ⓑ Ⓒ

Part 3

No.	ANSWER A B C D	No.	ANSWER A B C D
7	Ⓐ Ⓑ Ⓒ	9	Ⓐ Ⓑ Ⓒ Ⓓ
8	Ⓐ Ⓑ Ⓒ	10	Ⓐ Ⓑ Ⓒ Ⓓ
11		11	Ⓐ Ⓑ Ⓒ Ⓓ
12		12	Ⓐ Ⓑ Ⓒ Ⓓ
13		13	Ⓐ Ⓑ Ⓒ Ⓓ
14		14	Ⓐ Ⓑ Ⓒ Ⓓ

Part 4

No.	ANSWER A B C D	No.	ANSWER A B C D
15	Ⓐ Ⓑ Ⓒ Ⓓ	19	Ⓐ Ⓑ Ⓒ Ⓓ
16	Ⓐ Ⓑ Ⓒ Ⓓ	20	Ⓐ Ⓑ Ⓒ Ⓓ
17	Ⓐ Ⓑ Ⓒ Ⓓ		
18	Ⓐ Ⓑ Ⓒ Ⓓ		

READING SECTION

Part 5

No.	ANSWER A B C D
21	Ⓐ Ⓑ Ⓒ Ⓓ
22	Ⓐ Ⓑ Ⓒ Ⓓ
23	Ⓐ Ⓑ Ⓒ Ⓓ
24	Ⓐ Ⓑ Ⓒ Ⓓ

Part 6

No.	ANSWER A B C D
25	Ⓐ Ⓑ Ⓒ Ⓓ
26	Ⓐ Ⓑ Ⓒ Ⓓ
27	Ⓐ Ⓑ Ⓒ Ⓓ
28	Ⓐ Ⓑ Ⓒ Ⓓ

Part 7

No.	ANSWER A B C D	No.	ANSWER A B C D	No.	ANSWER A B C D
29	Ⓐ Ⓑ Ⓒ Ⓓ	33	Ⓐ Ⓑ Ⓒ Ⓓ	37	Ⓐ Ⓑ Ⓒ Ⓓ
30	Ⓐ Ⓑ Ⓒ Ⓓ	34	Ⓐ Ⓑ Ⓒ Ⓓ	38	Ⓐ Ⓑ Ⓒ Ⓓ
31	Ⓐ Ⓑ Ⓒ Ⓓ	35	Ⓐ Ⓑ Ⓒ Ⓓ	39	Ⓐ Ⓑ Ⓒ Ⓓ
32	Ⓐ Ⓑ Ⓒ Ⓓ	36	Ⓐ Ⓑ Ⓒ Ⓓ	40	Ⓐ Ⓑ Ⓒ Ⓓ